Sectarianism in Scotland

Sectarianism in Scotland

STEVE BRUCE, TONY GLENDINNING,
IAIN PATERSON AND MICHAEL ROSIE

Edinburgh University Press

© Steve Bruce, Tony Glendinning,
Iain Paterson and Michael Rosie, 2004

Edinburgh University Press Ltd
22 George Square, Edinburgh

Typeset in Bembo by
Hewer Text Ltd, Edinburgh, and
printed and bound in Great Britain by
Bell & Bain Ltd, Glasgow

A CIP record for this book is available from the British Library

ISBN 0 7486 1911 9 (paperback)

The right of Steve Bruce, Tony Glendinning,
Iain Paterson and Michael Rosie to be identified
as authors of this work has been asserted in accordance
with the Copyright, Designs and Patents Act 1988.

Contents

Preface

This book was born out of frustration with the dreadful quality of public debate about the importance of religious identity in modern Scotland. James MacMillan is a Catholic and he may be an excellent composer, but neither fact means that his views about the salience of sectarianism are well founded; yet, when he delivered his famous August 1999 speech, his claims that Catholics were still the victims of serious discrimination were given enormous prominence in the mass media. They were presented, not as the grumblings of one prominent musician, but as the case that must be answered. Officials of Nil by Mouth, a campaigning organisation set up to ameliorate Scotland's assumed problem, repeatedly present inaccurate statistics for the victims of sectarian murder and these are reported by serious newspapers as established fact. In 2002 the Church of Scotland decided to apologise for its sectarian past and, in order to make its apology all the more impressive, produced a description of the current state of sectarianism that repeated without any thought to their accuracy the same false statistics of sectarian violence. Jack McConnell, Scotland's First Minister, talks of sectarianism as Scotland's 'secret shame' but says nothing that suggests he or his speech-writers have troubled themselves to investigate the extent of the problem.

A few words about our backgrounds will help the reader to judge our credentials. Although it was followed quickly by Tom Galla-gher's much more detailed studies of sectarian politics in Glasgow and Edinburgh, Steve Bruce's 1986 *No Pope of Rome* was the first serious study of sectarianism since James Handley's pioneering work in the 1940s. Bruce has since published over 120 essays and eighteen books on religion and politics, many of them concerned with Northern Ireland and Scotland. Tony Glendinning is a trained mathematician who is now a senior lecturer in the Department of Sociology at the University of Aberdeen and he has collaborated with Bruce on the analysis of the 2001 Scottish Social Attitudes survey. Iain Paterson now works as a Senior Research Officer for Glasgow City Council. He was previously at the Department of Public Health at the University of Glasgow. His doctorate was awarded for the 2000 thesis 'Sectarianism in Scotland' and in 2001–3 he acted as Glasgow City Council's adviser for its research on sectarianism. Michael Rosie is a lecturer in sociology at the University of Edinburgh. He was awarded his doctorate for 'Religion and Sectarianism in Modern Scotland' in 2001 and has since been involved in the Leverhulme Trust-funded programme on 'Nation and Regions: Constitutional Change and Identity'. Of course, the views expressed here are ours and not those of our employers.

A note about the cover: the poster is a fake. Although it is often casually asserted that jobs in certain industries were advertised with the rider 'Catholics need not apply', we could find no example or good evidence that it ever occurred.

Acknowledgements

This study draws on a great deal of work that we have done severally and jointly over many years and a great many institutions and individuals have assisted us. Bruce's research on religion and politics has been funded at various times by the Economic and Social Research Council (ESRC), the British Academy and the Nuffield Foundation. The ESRC funded Bruce and Glendinning to insert a module of religion questions in the 2001 Scottish Social Attitudes survey (grant no. R000223485). It also supported the various Scottish Election surveys that we draw on.

The University of Aberdeen funded Paterson's doctoral research. The ESRC funded that of Rosie. The University of Aberdeen continues to support the research of Bruce and Glendinning.

The Chief Executive's Office of the Glasgow City Council gave us permission to analyse the data collected by NFO Social Research as part of the council's study of sectarianism. Chris Martin of NFO assisted with some technical advice. Frank Morris of the Registrar General's Census Office produced the data on religion and class from the 2001 Census data. Ian McLean of Nuffield College, Oxford, collected the data on the religious affiliations of Glasgow Labour councillors 1909–74. It was supplied to us by the UK Data Archive, University of Essex. Data on student numbers at Glasgow University were supplied by its duty archivist. The 2001 Scottish Social Attitudes survey was very ably administered by the National Centre for Social Research, Edinburgh. We would particularly like to thank Kerstin Hinds for her help with the questionnaire design.

Finally we would like to thank a number of colleagues who over the years have helped us in our understanding of sectarianism in Scotland: Prof. Tom Gallagher of the University of Bradford; Prof. David McCrone, Prof. Lindsay Paterson and Prof. Stewart Brown of the University of Edinburgh; Prof. John Curtice and Prof. Callum Brown of the University of Strathclyde; Dr David Seawright of the University of Leeds; Harry Reid, formerly editor of the *Herald*; and Dr Eric Kaufmann of Birkbeck College, University of London.

List of Tables

Abbreviations

CYMS	Catholic Young Men's Society
ESRC	Economic and Social Research Council
ILP	Independent Labour Party
IRA	Irish Republican Army
NHS	National Health Service
OPP	Orange and Protestant Party
PAS	Protestant Action Society
SCVO	Scottish Council for Voluntary Organisations
SNP	Scottish National Party
SPL	Scottish Protestant League
SRS	Scottish Reformation Society
SUP	Scottish Unionist Party
UDA	Ulster Defence Association
UFC	United Free Church
UVF	Ulster Volunteer Force

Introduction: Is Scotland Sectarian?

The Problem

The purpose of this book can be easily indicated by listing a variety of snippets taken randomly from our files:

- In a widely reported speech, Scots composer James MacMillan said: 'In many walks of life – in the workplace, in the professions, in academia, in the media, in politics and in sport – anti-Catholicism, even when it is not particularly malign, is as endemic as it is second nature.'[1]
- On 4 December 2000 Henry McLeish, Scotland's First Minister, and John Reid, the Westminster Parliament's Secretary of State for Scotland, met the Pope to commemorate the 400th anniversary of the pontifical Scots College in Rome.
- Scots novelist Andrew O'Hagan wrote: 'Scotland is a divisive bigoted society.'[2]
- In December 2002 Andy Goram, former goalkeeper for Glasgow Rangers Football Club and Scotland (and a man twice married to Catholic women), threatened to sue a radio commentator who accused him of hating Catholics.[3]
- In July 1999 newly released government documents from 1933 included a Cabinet memorandum considering repatriating im-

migrants from the Irish Free State who fell on poor relief. When asked to comment, Monsignor Tom Connelly, spokesman for the Catholic Church in Scotland, said: 'Thank God we've moved a long way. We're blessed today that the Irish are integrated into the country now, and we live happily alongside all other people.'[4]

- In March 2003 the Catholic Church's press officer issued a statement calling for an enquiry into the exclusion of Catholics from the Order of the Thistle. This ancient Order, membership of which is a gift of the Queen, has sixteen members at any time. The press officer described this as 'entrenched discrimination'. Prof. Tom Devine, a leading Scots Catholic academic, pointed out that until very recently members had been drawn from the aristocracy and that there had only ever been one woman member, and dismissed the statement as 'verging on paranoia'.[5]

- In an essay on sectarianism in modern Scotland, Prof. Patrick Reilly wrote: 'To ask if there is anti-Catholicism in Scotland is like asking if there are Frenchmen in Paris.'[6]

- Five years earlier Prof. Reilly responded to a book by Mary Hickman that had made extravagant claims for sectarianism in Scotland by saying her views 'do not really reflect the existing reality but are clichés based upon out-moded and obsolete facts which perhaps existed 50 years ago'.[7]

The Solution

The above shows, first, that Scots are divided about the extent of sectarianism and, secondly, that anecdotes can readily be found to support any position. We believe that sectarianism is important enough to be studied seriously. When Bruce was doing the research for *No Pope of Rome* in the early 1980s, he was frequently confronted with the view that to study bigots would 'just encourage them', as one now-very-well-known Scottish journalist, then just starting on her career, put it. Each of us has devoted considerable effort to studying various manifestations of sectarianism. We have collaborated on this book because we believe it is important that public discussion be informed by accurate information. That information has to be social scientific and it has to concern social phenomena. Swapping anecdotes about this factory where you could not work unless you were in the Orange Order or that promotion missed because you went to the wrong school gets us nowhere. No sensible person would judge the prevalence of smoking from the observations of his or her friends and relatives; our acquaintances might be unrepresentative. We appreciate that we would need large-scale surveys of people who were representative of the age or social class or region that interested us. The same is true of sectarianism. If we want to assert that Catholics suffer discrimination, we would first of all have to show that they are disadvantaged and the only way to do that is to collect and compare evidence about the socio-economic status of large numbers of Catholics and non-Catholics.

But information is not enough. We also need clarity of thought. What is dismaying about the quality of the current debate is the lack of care taken by many of those who express trenchant opinions. It is common to find people sliding, apparently unconsciously, from discussing drink-fuelled working-class thugs, to football fans generally, to generalisations about the social climate of Scotland. We need to distinguish carefully the various forms and expressions of sectarianism and what might count as evidence for any of them.

That final point can be extended to this general proposition: we need to separate the exotic from the typical. Consider the record of the 1930s anti-Catholic parties discussed in Chapter 2. It is, of course, important that we know about the rise of Alexander Ratcliffe's Scottish Protestant League and its brief flourish in Glasgow. But we also need to recognise that most Glaswegian Protestants did not vote for Ratcliffe and that in sheer size the number of Protestants who worked amicably with Catholics in trade unions and in the two labour parties of the period was vastly greater than the number who supported sectarian politics.

We also need always to assess evidence against its context. For example, James MacMillan presents the fact that in the 1990s the *Herald* employed John McLeod, a weekly columnist of Calvinist views who regularly denounced Romanism as a damnable heresy, as proof of the respectability and popularity of anti-Catholicism. By ignoring the context, MacMillan misses the point that the *Herald* columnists were selected first for their 'demographic' (hence there was also a 'young female Scot of Asian parents', a 'Catholic Scot of Irish descent' and 'a very young woman') and secondly for their ability to enrage readers so that they wrote to the paper's letters page.

McLeod was hired because he lived in Harris and because his views antagonised readers: that is, because he was exotic, not because he was typical. The great danger of argument by illustration and anecdote is that we notice the bizarre far more than we notice the ordinary. It may be dull and worthy, but, if we are going to make assertions about large groups of people, and large-scale social processes, and even whole countries, then we need to concentrate on the typical and not the extreme.

This book has three purposes. It presents first evidence about various social phenomena that might be glossed as sectarianism, then an overall assessment of the significance of sectarianism at the start of the twenty-first century, and finally an explanation of the changes of the last century. To state our conclusion at the outset, we believe that sectarianism has been much exaggerated; that Scotland's Catholics, most of whom are the descendants of Irish immigrants, now enjoy social, political and economic parity with non-Catholics; and that religion (or the ethnicity of one's ancestors) is no longer a major consideration in the lives of most Scots. In the matter of religious conflict, the history of Scotland is much closer to that of the United States or Australia than it is to that of Northern Ireland.

Readers may well disagree with that assessment, but we hope they will still read on, because, if this debate is to rise above ritual name-calling, we have to collaborate in addressing the evidence. Indeed, as well as delivering our assessment of sectarianism in modern Scotland, the book has the subsidiary purposes of clarifying the arguments and making known the many sets of statistical data that can be brought to bear on those arguments. If we cannot persuade our critics, we can at least help them focus their criticisms in a way that will allow testing.

We regard it as a welcome sign of maturity that Scots are now able to talk about sectarianism. We would like to ensure that future talk is informed by the best possible evidence and gets out of its current trough of hostile anecdotes, sweeping claims of victimhood and equally ill-founded apologies.

A few words of definition would be helpful. Rather than set up some foreign language, we will try to use everyday terms, but with a bit more precision. By 'sectarianism' we mean a widespread and shared culture of *improperly* treating people in terms of their religion. Of course there is a place for sectarian discrimination. We would think it odd if the Church of Rome did not enquire of intending clergy if they were Catholic or Protestant. We would think it inappropriate if a bus company enquired the same of intending bus-drivers.

Sectarianism usually has the narrower meaning in the British context of referring to relations between Protestants and Catholics. We will not be directly concerned with the status or treatment of non-Christians, though we do sometimes refer to it for purposes of comparison. Actually even that sentence requires clarification. Of course, we do not mean 'non-Christians' in the usual sense of the term, because most Scots are non-Christian. Most do not attend Christian churches, do not subscribe to the Apostles' Creed, and do not believe in the divinity of Christ. We mean people who are members of racial and ethnic groups that overwhelmingly still or traditionally adhere to some non-Christian faith.

It is worth adding here that, as in the common usage of the term, we are often concerned more with the identities that are assigned to people than with those they claim for themselves. Hence, when we talk of anti-Catholic discrimination, we mean disadvantaging people who are taken to be Catholic by the person doing the discriminating (because, for example, of having been educated in a Catholic school). Of course, many such people are not themselves Catholic in the sense that they are gymnasts, smokers or fathers.

A certain awkwardness stems from the fact that religion and ethnicity are mixed in this debate. Claims that Catholics are the victims of discrimination usually focus on the experience of Irish Catholic immigrants and their descendants. As we will explain in the first chapter, many Scots Catholics are not descended from Irish immigrants (and, equally well, a large proportion of Irish immigrants were not Catholics!). Where it matters we will distinguish between religious and ethnic labels, but it would be tiresome to overuse some cumbersome formula such as 'Catholics descended from Irish migrant forebears', so we will often be casual where precision is not required.

Throughout the book we have tried to distinguish between inherent disadvantage, effective discrimination and bigotry. It may be that Irish Catholic migrants were slow to prosper because of a lack of capital, low levels of education and an absence of industrial skills – features they possessed that were quite independent of the hostility of native Scots. It may also be that such bigotry as we find did little to produce effective discrimination. It may have had some effect in encouraging migrants to form a relatively isolated community but still have had little effect in terms of denying rights or opportunities to Catholics. Or we may conclude that bigotry created discrimination and that internal disadvantages were of no consequence. Whatever the outcome, we have to begin by supposing the links between these three phenomena need to be examined.

Notes

1. J. MacMillan, 'Scotland's shame', in T. Devine (ed.), *Scotland's Shame? Bigotry and Sectarianism in Modern Scotland* (Edinburgh: Mainstream, 2000), p. 15. We note rather ruefully that this collection of essays, which was meant to subject the MacMillan thesis to rational and dispassionate scrutiny, has itself become a shibboleth. Those commentators who think that sectarianism is still a powerful force regularly allow their subconscious minds to augment their arguments by dropping the question mark from the first part of the title.
2. A. O'Hagan, 'Into the ferment', in Devine (ed.), *Scotland's Shame?*, p. 25.
3. *Sun*, 15 December 2002.
4. *Sunday Mail*, 18 July 1999.
5. *Herald*, 10 March 2003.
6. P. Reilly, 'Kicking with the left foot: being Catholic in Scotland', in Devine (ed.), *Scotland's Shame?*, p. 29.
7. *Herald*, 20 March 1996.

1 The Nineteenth Century

Introduction

The past may be another country but it is where we must start if we are to make sense of the present. In this chapter we explain the religious composition of Scotland, trace the pattern of Irish immigration and evaluate early modern responses to Catholicism. In the next chapter we consider sectarianism in the twentieth century.

In the second half of the sixteenth century, the unity of European Christendom was fractured by that series of religious conflicts we now think of as the Protestant Reformation. Although the Reformation was more popular in Scotland than in England, its impact was uneven. In parts of Aberdeenshire local magnates were able to resist change. The rest of the English-speaking Lowlands rapidly became Protestant, but the Gaelic-speaking Highlanders, protected from innovation by their geographical isolation, were largely untouched by this revolution in religion, culture and social organisation.[1] The Highlands remained pagan, Roman Catholic or, if the milder Protestantism of the English Church had penetrated, Episcopalian.[2]

Differences between Highlands and Lowlands would gradually have been eroded by the greater economic power of the south; the demand for livestock, for example, was bringing the Highlands more and more into the Lowlands economy. But the distinctive culture and society of the Highlands was brought to an abrupt end by the failure of the attempts, in 1715 and 1745, to use the Highlands as a base for the restoration of the Catholic Stewart dynasty to the British throne. The supporters of the Hanoverian monarchy and the Protestant faith responded to the two Jacobite risings with a programme of systematic social reconstruction. The symbols of the old feudal society were outlawed, and the clan chiefs were stripped of their legislative powers and their weapons. To encourage the speedy incorporation of the Highlands into the Lowlands economy, and to ensure that any subsequent rebellion could be more easily quashed, metalled roads were built into the Highlands.[3]

The Highland chiefs, many of whom had extensive contacts with Edinburgh, London and the continental capitals, quickly acquiesced in this reconstruction and, as part of their adjustment, adopted the Protestant religion of the established Presbyterian Church of Scotland. This did not lead immediately to the enthusiastic attachment of the Highland people to the Reformed faith. The people of pre-industrial societies usually follow their masters in religion, as in everything else, but the shredding of traditional ties of dependency and loyalty meant that the common people could no longer be herded into a new ideology: they had to be persuaded into Presbyterianism. That was not easy when there were few Gaelic speakers to fill the vacancies in Highland parishes. In remote areas clerical provision was extremely thin: the whole island of Lewis was a single parish and the parish of Ardnamurchan was ninety miles from one end to the other.

That the Highlands and Islands had by the end of the nineteenth century become a stronghold of a particularly rigorous evangelical Protestantism is largely due to the Clearances. When the Highland chiefs still had a military role, they had good reason to keep the land stocked with people; their power was a function of the size of the army they could raise. When the clan system became redundant, it suited them better to become landlords pure and simple. Status in Edinburgh and London now depended on income from rents and they could not be raised while the land was let to a complex pyramid of tenants and sub-tenants for nominal sums and military service. Tenants had to become efficient farmers and peasants had to become labourers.[4] The speed of change varied from place to place, usually in relation to the wealth of the chief. The wealthiest (the Duke of Argyll, for example) were the slowest to act. But the general principles were those seen all over Europe: enclose the common land and get rid of the people. The people were moved to the coast to make way for sheep.

It is common for major economic and social upheavals to trigger radical changes of world view. Changes in the economy of medieval Europe produced a large pool of dispossessed and insecure individuals; many of them joined radical religious movements that preached the imminent end of the world. In the late eighteenth century, the industrialisation of England produced the Methodist movement. In the 1970s the decline of the hacienda system of agriculture and the rapid growth of mega-cities in Latin America provided fertile ground for the spread of Pentecostal Protestantism in what had been a solidly Catholic culture. In the Scottish Highlands, clearance produced a market for radical evangelicalism. Certainly contemporary commentators saw evangelicalism as a response to social change: 'It is well-known that no itinerant preacher ever gained a footing among the highlanders, till recent changes in their situations and circumstances made way for fanaticism.'[5] That author was a Jacobite romantic who mourned the passing of quaint Highland superstitions, but his view is supported by a moderate Presbyterian who liked the change almost as little: 'the recent degradation and misery of the people have predisposed their minds to imbibe these pestiferous delusions to which they fly for consolation under their sufferings.'[6]

Evangelicalism was popular with the Highlanders because it offered an explanation of their problems (sin) and a solution (piety). It also allowed the people to criticise their landlords and the moderate clergy who supported them. Kennedy's succinct judgement of the ministers of Ross-shire can stand for the views of many Highlanders about their clergy: they 'cared not to affect much Godliness and were not suspected of any'.[7] But many ministers compounded their sins by trying to justify clearance.

The timing of the Highland conversion left Scotland divided. The Highlanders joined the mainstream of Scottish religion just in time to leave it again. At the same time as those north and west of the Highland line were becoming conservative evangelicals, much of the Lowlands was becoming liberal. When the national Church split in

1843, one-third of its clergy and congregations left to form the Free Church and the Highlands and Islands were very firmly in the Free Church camp. And at every subsequent reunion, the Highlands were always in the conservative rump that insisted on maintaining the old ways.

We can summarise the situation around the middle of the nineteenth century as follows. Most Scots were Presbyterians. And most of those adhered to the state Presbyterian church, but a growing number belonged to various Seceder[8] churches. There were small pockets of Catholicism in Banff and Buchan and in some of the western isles. There were also small groups of Episcopalians.

Irish Immigration and Anti-Catholicism

There had always been seasonal traffic between the north-east of Ireland and Scotland, but in the second half of the nineteenth century that changed. Economic hardship in Ireland (particularly the potato famine of 1849) and economic opportunity in Scotland, either in the new industries or in replacing in agriculture Scots who had moved to the cities, turned mobility into permanent migration. Bishop Hay's census of 1780 mentions only 6,600 Roman Catholics below the Highland line.[9] In 1795 there were only fifty Catholics in Glasgow. By 1829 there were 25,000 and in 1843 almost twice that number. Edinburgh in 1829 had some 14,000 Catholics where thirty years earlier there had been no more than 1,000.[10]

As Joseph Devine, Bishop of Motherwell, notes, the pattern and dating of Irish Catholic settlement can be discerned from the dates when Catholic parishes were founded: Rutherglen was 1851; Wishaw, Chapelhall and Lanark were 1859; Carfin 1862; Mossend 1868; Shotts 1868; Newmains 1871; Cleland and Whifflet 1874; Motherwell 1875; Blantyre 1877; Longriggend and Cambuslang 1878; Baillieston and Glenboig 1880; Uddingston 1883; Cadzow 1883; Shieldmuir 1891; Langloan 1892 and Newton 1894.[11]

Irish migration provided both the object and the stimulus for anti-Catholicism; not all the migrants were Catholics. Graham Walker estimates that between a quarter and a third of the Ulster migrants were Protestants and many of them were Orangemen who brought with them a culture of anti-Catholicism.[12] Orangeism had first been brought to Scotland by soldiers of the Scottish Fencibles sent to

Ireland in 1798 to help quell the rebellion.[13] It fairly quickly spread through the western and central industrial Lowlands. It appealed because it gave men who lived a hard and unrewarding life, often new to the impersonality of the town and the factory, a place in which they could develop their sense of self-worth and self-confidence. Those who were masters of very little found reward in becoming Worshipful Masters of their lodges. The values of popular egalitarian Protestantism provided an ideological core for a welcoming fraternal organisation. Like many such fraternities, the Order allowed workers to further each other's interests. Recruitment to small enterprises was invariably by word of mouth and personal recommendation. Foremen would use their influence to make sure that relatives and friends secured the best jobs. Where formal credentials were unnecessary, people promoted the interests of those most like themselves, and paternalistic factory-owners were usually happy to recruit workers through extended family networks.

That most of the Irish immigrants were poor, ill-educated and lacking industrial skills meant that they entered the Scottish labour market at the bottom. Some Protestant workers benefited from them staying there and used their networks of influence (among which was the local church and the local Orange lodge) as a vehicle for excluding the newcomers. Some employers, according to Callum Brown, 'used patronage of the Orange Lodge as a form of company paternalism with which to create Protestant worker identification with management and this undermined trades-union organisation'.[14] The Orange Order certainly had a considerable presence among the craft workers in the shipyards at the start of the twentieth century, but how widespread and effective was religious discrimination is not clear. It is possible that the deliberate exclusion of Catholics has been exaggerated. The historical record is certainly short of evidence. The one example that recurs is Bairds, Ironmasters of Gartsherrie. The Bairds were paternalists who built modern houses for their workers and had them periodically inspected. Prizes were given for the best kept. Those whose houses were habitually dirty were fined. The Bairds were evangelical Presbyterians. They built the parish church and employed a missionary to badger the workers during the week. Remarkable for continuous process manufacture, the Baird furnaces were damped down on the Sabbath so that nothing should inhibit church attendance. Graham Walker suggests that Bairds used Orange lodge contacts to recruit workers from Ulster.[15] But Handley, who might be expected to distinguish between Catholic and Protestant workers, refers to those who worked at Bairds simply as 'Irishmen' and mentions 'the Irish ironworkers of Shotts'.[16] Campbell thinks there were fewer Catholics employed at Gartsherrie than at other local ironworks, but that suggests that Catholics were employed in the industry and that the Bairds did employ Catholics.[17]

Whatever part discrimination played in this fate, there is no doubt that Catholic Irish migrants were largely found in 'that army of general labourers which serviced a wide variety of industries',[18] but they did not have a monopoly of unskilled work. Hordes of Scots migrants from the country (especially from the Highlands) were also drawn into the industrial world as brute labour. Irish Catholics were less well equipped than many Scots, but they competed within the same labour market. There were Catholic miners and Orange miners.[19] They were not, like white and black in South Africa or in the southern states of the USA, in entirely segregated markets that operated with quite different terms and conditions.

Not surprisingly, because this was the attraction, the arrival of the Irish in Scotland coincided with the great wave of urban expansion and industrialisation. The long-term result of industrial growth was massively increased prosperity, but the early stages were often extremely unpleasant. Peasant life may not have been the bucolic paradise imagined by the romantic critics of industrial life, but it was familiar and secure. The life of the industrial worker was often harsh and cruel. Those native Scots who found their conditions uncongenial could observe that the Irish and the problems of industrialisation arrived at the same time and some blamed the former for the latter. A very small part of this association was accurate: some mine-owners used Irish labourers as 'scabs' to break the emerging power of organised labour.[20] But most of it was scapegoating. Distressed people like to find a simple cause of their problems. For some native Scots, that was the Irish.

The conflict was not only economic; it was also religious and cultural in the wider sense. It is worth pausing here and stressing an important point that is often forgotten in modern discussions of religion: people used to believe it! When few of us have any church connection and the main Christian churches have dispensed with large parts of their historic creed (for example, heaven still exists for the European Christian but hell is barely mentioned), it is hard for us to imagine a world in which people actually believe in a creator God, the divinity of Jesus, the revealed nature of the Bible and the sacramental power of the Church. We tend to suppose that those who fight over whether the Pope has privileged access to the mind of God must really be quarrelling about something else. Because it does not move us, it could not move them. Although it takes some effort, we must think ourselves into the position of people who believe in heaven and hell and who suppose that possessing the right faith is essential to secure their position in the first of those and not the second. Of course, there were charlatans who protested to a faith they did not possess. And there were people whose strong commit-ment to their faith was driven in part by its ability to make their base motives seem more honourable. But most of those who disdained the religion of others did so because they genuinely believed it wrong and dangerously wrong. Protestant parents who feared a child marrying a Catholic and Catholic parents who refused to send a child to a predominantly Protestant school were not mindless bigots; they were loving parents anxious to ensure that they met their children again in heaven.

The Catholic migrants from Ireland were especially Roman Catholic. A century of being surrounded by evangelical Protestants had muted the distinctive features of Scottish Catholicism and made it more 'Protestant'. In contrast, the styles of worship and the relations between clergy and people among the Irish were seen as vulgar Catholicism. Scots read the emphasis on ritual as evidence that the Catholic Church was indifferent to the morals of its parishioners. They took the laity's obedience to their Church as proof of subservience. They regarded the social characteristics of the impo-verished Irish, not as consequences of their economic position but as a result of having the wrong religion. Accurately described but exaggerated differences were constructed into self-serving invidious stereotypes. Protestants Scots presented themselves as loyal, hard-working, diligent, literate, temperate and self-disciplined. They depicted the Irish as treacherous, slothful, illiterate, alcoholic and priest-ridden. The interesting thing about these constructs was that they were fully shared by old Scots Catholics.[21]

Prior to 1850, Irish priests had not been welcomed by the Scottish church, which feared being colonised by the much larger church in Ireland.[22] Although quickly overwhelmed by the Irish influx, the Scottish church officials were reluctant to recruit Irish priests and few attained senior posts before the late nineteenth century.[23] Relations were not helped by Scottish priests operating a system of seat renting in chapels to separate the 'respectable' Scots from the 'rough' Irish, and tensions were only lessened after the appointment of the neutrally English Charles Eyre to the Archdiocese of Glasgow in 1869. Thereafter, Irish priests came to dominate in the industrial areas out of necessity, leaving only the northern dioceses traditionally Scottish in character. The reception the native Catholic laity gave the immigrants was at best lukewarm. Speaking of Britain as a whole, E. H. Hunt states that 'native Roman Catholics did little to welcome their pauperised co-religionists – the division of class, culture and nationality proved greater than the bonds of shared religion'.[24]

We will use one example of anti-Catholic action to make some general points about the social location of support for militant Protestantism in the early nineteenth century. In 1829, the British government decided to remove most of the legal obstacles to Roman Catholics enjoying full citizenship. There were vigorous protests from some Scots who thought the authoritarianism of the Catholic Church a threat to democracy and a close examination of those brings some important divisions to light.[25]

First, there not much elite support for such campaigns. Although Glasgow town council petitioned against emancipation, the position was decided by the narrowest of majorities: 10 for, 9 against and 2 abstentions. More concerted opposition came from the skilled working class. The incorporated trades guilds in the west coast opposed emancipation unanimously or with very little dissent.

Second, there was a regional bias in opinion. While the Glasgow guilds were opposed to liberalisation, those of the east coast were in favour. The nine guilds of Dundee approved the measure and petitioned Parliament in support. The guilds of Arbroath were among the first to approve. Those of Aberdeen and Edinburgh seemed evenly divided and most chose to make no representation. A similar regional bias can be seen in the reaction of the churches. The Glasgow Presbytery of the Church of Scotland was more opposed to emancipation than was the Edinburgh Presbytery.

The third point concerns a theological division: generally the more conservative Presbyterians were most vocal in their opposition. But even the conservatives were not united in their attitude to Catholics. There was a group of Church of Scotland evangelicals led by Thomas Chalmers who argued in favour of ending Catholic disabilities. This came from a mix of motives. In part there was a genuine commitment to egalitarianism but there was also a missionary interest. Chalmers believed that civil and legal restrictions on Catholics only made them contemptuous of a faith that could need such support. Creating a level playing field was, he believed, a precondition for the conversion of the Irish.[26]

There was also some support for increased toleration of Catholics from the smaller Presbyterian churches, which were being driven to reconsider their position by self-interest and failure. The Secession Church had been founded on the principle of state support for the one true religion (which its members claimed to have). As it became obvious that they had failed to supplant the Church of Scotland, they became more sympathetic to the cause of religious liberty. Some conservative spokesmen were able to distinguish between tolerating varieties of Protestantism and allowing the same grace to Roman Catholics, but that ambivalence in their own position, allied in some cases with the Chalmers' position that religious liberty would improve the chances of converting Catholics, was enough to prevent the conservative Protestants presenting a coherent and committed united front against the Emancipation Act. The net result was that, despite some noise, the Catholic Emancipation Act was passed.

Victorian No Popery
In the absence of survey evidence, it is very difficult to gauge the popularity of anti-Catholicism, but we can use the careers of the three best-known protagonists of the Victorian era – James Begg, John Hope and Jacob Primmer – to illustrate its decline. Each was concerned primarily with the religious quarrel, but their stances readily translated into anti-Irish sentiment simply because the Irish were the largest and most obviously visible carriers of the dangerous heresy of Romanism.

James Begg (1808–83) was minister of Edinburgh's Newington Free Church and, in the middle of the nineteenth century, the Free Kirk's best-known anti-Popery agitator. Along with other Free

Church leaders, Begg set up the Scottish Reformation Society (SRS) in 1851. For Begg, Catholicism was dangerous on two grounds: it was obviously a false religion and it was also imperialist. It represented 'a studied and diabolical attempt to stamp out religion . . . everything which would lead the soul to Christ was either completely denied or destructively perverted'.[27] Rome represented the heart of an anti-scriptural political conspiracy that aimed at world domination. Small Protestant nations such as Scotland were a crucial bulwark of liberty against the machinations of Popery. The essence of Begg's view of Rome was encapsulated in one of his speeches:

> . . . considered theologically, it was the Antichrist of Scripture, the deadly enemy of the Gospel of Christ . . . considered politically, it was a great gigantic system of despotism . . . considered socially, it was a most complicated curse to any country or neighbourhood in which it prevailed . . . Considered historically, it presented a series of the most fearful degradations of man, and insults to God, which history had ever exhibited.[28]

Begg's paranoia was not baseless. His estimate of Catholic power in Britain was wildly inaccurate, but his assessment of the ambitions of the Catholic Church was a reasonable reading of the Church's own pronouncements. In the nineteenth century the Church held that it was the true Church and that Protestantism was a dangerous heresy. Where the Church was dominant, it routinely opposed the extension of the franchise and the evolution of liberal democratic politics; where it was in control (the papal states, for example), it banned them.

It is difficult to know with certainty whom Begg represented. Certainly the *Bulwark*, the journal of his, was widely read by the Free Church clergy and laity, and Begg was elected Moderator of the Free Church in 1865. Yet he was in many ways a maverick. He was a Conservative in a church that strongly supported the Liberal Party, but he sometimes criticised capitalists and defended the interests of the working class with what later would be called a 'social gospel'. One reason for being a little cautious in allowing Begg to stand for the entire Free Church is a major 1881 book produced by Begg's protégé Revd James Wylie.[29] To celebrate the achievements of the Free Church, Wylie compiled a collection of biographies of seventy Free Kirk worthies. We can presume that Wylie would have been keen to record anti-Catholicism where he could find it: he found it in only a handful of his celebrities.[30]

Begg's near-equivalent in the Church of Scotland was a layman. Edinburgh solicitor John Hope (1807–93) was, like Begg, an active Conservative. Hope found religion in his early thirties and embraced temperance and anti-Popery with the enthusiasm of the convert. In 1854 he helped to form the Scottish Protestant Association as a Kirk-focused rival to the SRS. Although Hope admired Begg's position on Popery, he viewed the SRS as a Free Church organisation and complained that, though its members were 'very active and talked much . . . they did not come down with the money, proposing to make everything pay for itself, and to publish tracts at . . . a price beyond the working-classes'.[31] From a wealthy background, Hope did 'come down with the money' for his causes. After success with his British League of Junior Abstainers, Hope took up No Popery. He produced cheap pamphlets in bulk and organised public meetings, evening classes and essay competitions. Although a member of the Church of Scotland, Hope acted independently and ecumenically. Hope saw the world in the simple terms of good versus evil, right versus wrong. Protestantism was self-evidently true and Catholicism false; all that was required to bring people to Christ was to educate them in the truths of Protestantism and, crucially, in the errors and dangers of Popery.

Despite his wealth, status and enthusiasm, Hope's schemes often foundered through ambivalence or hostility on the part of Presbyterian ministers. He complained: 'I fear we can look for nothing from public men, and that the children must be trained up in Protestant knowledge before the country will right itself.'[32] Here Hope had considerable success: in 1873 he had almost 500 young people enrolled in his No Popery classes. These classes were crucial in keeping the critique of Catholicism alive at a time when mainstream Presbyterianism was losing interest in it. That loss of enthusiasm was demonstrated in 1859 when the Church of Scotland's Committee on Popery – founded in 1851 after the 'Papal Aggression' scare – was wound up and merged with the Home Missions Board. The deeply disappointed Hope was never again to be active in the official work of the Church.

If the Kirk's committee shuffling hints at it, events after Hope's death clearly show the increasing marginality of anti-Catholicism.

Hope died wealthy and without dependants, and left his extended family nothing, leaving his entire estate to combating Rome and drink. Between £1,000 and £1,500 was to be spent annually to promote total abstinence, with the remainder to be used in 'the dissemination of knowledge regarding the anti-scriptural nature of Popery, in arousing people to a sense of the evils of Popery, [and] in efforts towards the conversion of Roman Catholics'.[33] Hope's relatives had been unsympathetic to his views while he was alive; they were furious at this post-mortem insult. Unable to challenge Hope's will on legal grounds, they claimed that his mind had been unbalanced. They argued that being so fixated on temperance and Popery as to prefer those causes to one's own blood was itself strong evidence of mental imbalance. There was no real doubt over Hope's sanity and, had the suit been threatened forty years earlier, the Trustees could have been confident that the relatives had no case. In 1893 the Trustees could not be sure that they could find a jury in Presbyterian Edinburgh sufficiently sympathetic with Hope's causes. They settled out of court.

Further evidence of the decline of anti-Catholicism can be found in the career of Jacob Primmer (1842–1914).[34] Primmer was a working-class graduate of Hope's evening classes who, with Hope's assistance, entered Edinburgh University to study for the ministry. During the summer holidays he toured southern England as a subscription agent for the SRS, an experience that revealed a talent as a 'controversialist' and confirmed him on a path that was to bring notoriety, frustrated ambition and failure. He spent one summer assisting a sick minister in Westray, Shetland. When the minister died, members of the congregation said they would be happy to elect him as a permanent replacement. The Earl of Zetland's agent appointed a less contentious candidate. When he graduated, he was appointed as a missioner to the small Banffshire fishing village of Gardenstown – a post that gave none of the security of a parish ministry. Although he successfully built a new church, Primmer's trenchant views offended many of the congregation and he was moved on, to Townhill, where he embarked on a thirty years' war with his congregation, the Presbytery of Dunfermline and the General Assembly. Primmer's attacks on Popery and Irish nationalism alienated some of the managers and patrons of Townhill Mission and his enthusiastic denunciation of the demon drink alienated the rest. At one point relations were so bad that members of the Dunfermline Presbytery offered Primmer £100 if he would resign.[35] He could not plausibly be sacked for believing with conviction things that the Church notionally held in common, but, without the financial security of a settled position, Primmer's income was vulnerable. It is a measure of his unpopularity that the Home Missions Board regularly withheld a sizeable proportion of his stipend. Each year Primmer appealed to the General Assembly for full payment of his salary, and each year the assembly rejected his appeals. In 1895 he lost by 89 votes to 44; in 1896 by 256 votes to 106.

Primmer was unpopular because he was a trouble-maker. He loved the thrill of the outdoor meeting that might be disrupted by heckling or worse. In 1888, alongside two Kirk ministers and a banner inscribed 'Christ Our King and Covenant', Primmer addressed an open-air meeting at Hill of Beath in Fife that reputedly attracted a crowd of 6,000. Thus started a fourteen-year series of tours around Scotland to address the supposedly pressing menace of Popery. Primmer's interests and fixations were a perfect encapsulation of Victorian anti-Catholicism: the sexual immorality of convent, priest and confessional; the pagan symbolism and rituals of Romanism; the licentiousness of drunken Irish Catholics; and the Romanist political conspiracy against the British Empire and Protestant liberty. In these views he differed little from Begg or Hope, but his style was different and the tide was running out. Begg was the studious theologian, producing minutely argued attacks on Popery. Hope was the quiet bureaucrat, ensuring that many were educated in the controversy. Primmer was a showman: a spectacular tub-thumper who attracted hooligans like a trawler draws seagulls in its wake. He took to saving a few souvenirs from the stones that were regularly thrown at him: he painted the place and the date on each. Many Presbyterians thought him coarse and vulgar: someone who pandered to the least appealing aspects of human nature. Which was exactly what attracted his audiences: controversial public meetings were a form of cheap entertainment and the prospect of some violence added considerably to the appeal. But he was operating in a shrinking market. Fewer and fewer people cared passionately about religion, and, despite attempts by some militant Protestants to link the Papacy and the Kaiser, the real aggression of the First World War made the abstraction of 'papal aggression' seem somewhat remote.

A careful reading of Primmer's biography shows one repeated theme that is vital to assessing the power of anti-Catholicism. We could take Primmer as representative of Presbyterian attitudes and fail to notice that he was usually campaigning against some error of his Church of Scotland colleagues. He agitated against the images that appeared in the renovation of St Giles' in Edinburgh. He campaigned against the Kirk's hymnal (because it contained 'popish error and idolatry'). He denounced the General Assembly as 'the hydra-headed, traitorous oligarchy'.[36] Even Primmer knew he was losing.

Measuring Hostility

The orthodox view of Protestant–Catholic relations in the nineteenth century is that they varied between exploitation and grudging acceptance at best and attempts at expulsion and regular violence at worst. While not entirely inaccurate, this may be somewhat misleading. Much of the impression created by a writer such as Handley depends on the order in which he presents his material. To give one example, Handley says:

> When the council of Glasgow discontinued the ringing of bells on Guy Fawkes' Day, much to the chagrin of the *Scottish Guardian* [a small anti-Catholic paper], it consoled itself with the reflection that the public hoardings were plastered in compensation on that day with the anti-Catholic slogans of the zealots.[37]

Quite reasonably Handley constructs the sentence in a way that gives pride of place to his main interest: he is describing popular anti-Catholicism. A different impression would have been created had we described the same thing as:

> The *Scottish Guardian* was left to console itself with the fact that its supporters daubed anti-Catholic slogans on hoardings when Glasgow Council ignored its wishes and ceased celebrating Guy Fawkes Day.

In this version the main event is the council's decision to stop commemorating the foiling of a Catholic attempt to destroy the

government. What the *Scottish Guardian* thinks about the change has
been put in its proper place: a peripheral reaction. The same point
can be made about the way Tom Gallagher describes Protestant
opposition to the Maynooth grant. For fifty years the British
government had been sporadically giving financial assistance to
the Catholic college at Maynooth in Ireland. In 1845 it decided
to make the grant regular and thus prevent it occasioning opposition
every time it was debated. Gallagher dwells on opposition to the
move in a way that distracts us from the fact that the militant
Protestants had lost the argument.[38] Similarly with vocal opposition
to the restoration of the Catholic Church's hierarchy in England.
The protests are described in detail; we overlook the fact that the
protestors lost the argument. The Catholic Church was allowed to
create a full church structure.[39]

Much else in Handley's account can be reread in the same way and
we dwell on it because Handley is very often the only source cited by
modern commentators who are impressed by how bad things used to
be. In his many accounts of popular sectarian disturbances, the
behaviour of the authorities is mentioned only in subordinate
clauses. This has the effect of minimising the extent to which
Scottish elites of various sorts either failed to support popular
anti-Catholicism or deliberately acted to constrain it. One of a band
of public showmen who made a living from publicly and floridly
denouncing the evils of Popery styled himself 'the Angel Gabriel'.
Handley's main interest is that Gabriel drew crowds. Only in passing
does he mention that the Greenock police arrested him as a trouble-
maker.[40] In discussing sectarian rioting in Patrick in 1875 Handley
notes that the Orange Order asked for its members to be enrolled as
special constables. That the Provost declined the offer is mentioned
but may be missed on a casual reading. When a minister, McColl,
had a pulpit built outside the Free Church in Bridgegate in Glasgow
in 1860 so that he could hector the public, he attracted very large and
unruly crowds. The police dispersed the crowds.[41]

Mention of the Angel Gabriel allows us to insert an important
aside: it reminds us that much of the sectarian violence of the
nineteenth century was reciprocal. It would be a great mistake to
suppose that Irish Catholics were as powerless against Protestant
bigots as blacks in Mississippi before the civil-rights movement of the
1960s were against the Ku Klux Klan. As Donald McRaild's

accounts of trouble in nineteenth-century Cumbria show, Irish navvies were quite capable of looking after themselves.[42] In 1872, William Murphy, an itinerant militant Protestant speaker, was beaten to death by Irish miners in Workington. Another preacher, John Kensit Snr, died as a result of injuries received when he was attacked in Birkenhead in 1902.[43]

It is worth considering the posture of the Scottish press. To illustrate the taken-for-granted nature of invidious stereotypes, Handley cites some examples of court-reporting from the *North British Daily Mail*: 'Yesterday at the Central Police Court, an ape-faced, small-headed Irishman . . . A middle-aged, malicious-looking Irishman . . . Two surly-looking sons of the Emerald Isle . . . Pat O'Shannan, a startled-looking Irish tailor, with a cruel Tipperary visage.'[44] But we should note that the same paper used equally intemperate language to describe the Protestant poor and it wrote of 'that blustering and foolish body, the No Popery agitators'.[45] Most works that discuss nineteenth-century bigotry (and our previous work is guilty of this) do not do much to assess its prevalence. To show that there was a lot of very nasty anti-Catholicism about we quote small circulation partisan journals that were founded to promote anti-Catholicism. Handley, for example, quotes extensively from the *Scottish Guardian* and the *Bulwark*. This can leave the impression that most Scots were positively anti-Catholic and anti-Irish. The problem of representativeness can be seen clearly if we imagine that future historians decide to illustrate the views of capitalism prevalent in 1970s Britain by quoting from the Communist Party's *Morning Star* and the *Socialist Worker*. Such quotations would illustrate but they would not represent.

Handley's own work can often sustain an alternative reading. In 1859, a minor scandal arose in the staffing of a lunatic asylum, the Crichton Royal Institution in Dumfries. The assistant matron, who had converted to Catholicism, was denied the right, promised to her before her conversion, to take over as matron when the post became free. Fifty Edinburgh worthies, over half of them ministers of the Free Church, petitioned against her appointment. That testifies to the anti-Catholicism of many in the Free Church. But equally important is that the *Scotsman*, the largest circulation Edinburgh paper, denounced this petition as 'a most painfully humiliating exhibition of modern Protestantism and an exceedingly weak sample

of the common sense of the Scottish metropolis'.[46] Over the second
half of the nineteenth century, the *Scotsman* repeatedly 'doused the
fervour of the extremists with streams of ice-cold logic from its
leaders'.[47] It castigated the Greenock Poor Law authorities for
refusing the local priest the chance to provide religious instruction
for Catholic children in the poorhouse. In a series of articles on
poverty in Edinburgh, the *Scotsman* countered the assertions of anti-
Catholic campaigners by making an unflattering comparison between Scots and Irish poor:

> Whenever among the females in all parts of Edinburgh you meet
> with those in whose whole appearance their wretched occupation
> is inscribed in unmistakable characters – you find them to be
> Scottish. On the other hand, in the lowest hovels occupied by the
> Irish . . . you do not find these appearances . . . and while an
> unpolite Irishman is a rarity, an Irish woman not polite is, I
> suspect, something that has not yet been discovered in this
> world . . . The dirty Romanist family generally wash their faces
> once a week and go to the idolatrous mass. The dirty Protestants
> will not wash their faces nor go to the next street to hear the glad
> tidings of the gospel.[48]

The writer makes no secret of his religious beliefs but can hardly be
accused of maintaining invidious anti-Irish stereotypes.

The *Scotsman*'s counterpart in Glasgow, the *Herald*, is also mentioned a number of times by Handley as either countering anti-Irish
stereotypes or acting so as to dampen animosity. In 1878, when the
Catholic Church in Scotland was permitted by the Pope to create a
full hierarchical structure, the *Glasgow Herald* judged that it would
give the Pope pleasure and do Scotland no harm.[49] In 1883, during a
time of unusual tension, the *Glasgow Herald* wrote of one public
meeting: 'the Rev. Mr Rossborough delivered a rather inflammatory
speech to which, in the present excited state of the public mind, we
do not deem it desirable to give publicity.'[50] Handley notes that 'by
the last quarter or so of the nineteenth century newspapers had for
the most part dropped their hostile attitude towards the religion of
the majority of the immigrants' and that, when the Catholic
hierarchy was restored, what excited the bigots 'evoked only
moderate response' from the mainstream of Scottish opinion.[51]

One very specific example of elite unwillingness to encourage bigotry concerns what we might, with little exaggeration, call 'evangelical porn': convent inspection. Celibacy has always divided Catholics and Protestants. Catholics see it as proof of especial piety. Protestants believe that sexual urges are universal and that the best way to control them is to allow a legitimate outlet: monogamous marriage. Catholics priests and nuns say that their faith allows them to transcend their animal urges. Because they cannot believe in that faith, Protestants suppose that apparently celibate clerics are actually perverts. That was the logic behind the anti-Catholic campaigns against the institution of the confessional (where male priests supposedly encouraged women to talk about sex) and the convent (where women were supposedly molested). In the spirit of modern tabloid newspapers that describe sex crimes in rather too much detail, anti-Catholic agitators supported their demands for government intervention with lengthy pamphlets that described what supposedly went on behind the convent walls. Our point is that, while we may take the market for such lurid tales as *The Awful Confessions of Maria Monk* as evidence of Protestant bigotry, we should also remember that the government did not act on them.

It is also worth drawing attention to a common feature of sectarian relations in the nineteenth century that has considerable significance for our story and will be considered in detail in the last chapter. In 1852 the magistrates in Greenock, which had witnessed considerable mob violence, sentenced to just sixty days in gaol a man who had attempted to kill a policeman. When the violence persisted, the government intervened to suspend the magistrates and the town clerk, and replace them with a paid professional magistrate.[52] Restated in general terms, that example was repeated frequently: in some places there was some sympathy for aggressive anti-Catholicism but local preferences were invariably over-ruled by more cosmopolitan elites who regarded social order as more important than local values.

Education
The history of Catholic schooling is important because it allows us to see all three elements of our account. It shows the Catholic Church (and its immigrant people) displaying heroic self-reliance but also limiting itself to the not-very-extensive resources of those people. It

shows some Protestants encouraging popular militant anti-Catholic campaigns. And it shows the Protestant ruling class behaving decently: ignoring its militants and doing its best to improve the Catholic community while trying to accommodate the wishes of the Catholic Church to retain control over the education of its people.

John Knox's blueprint for a Presbyterian kingdom included compulsory national education. It took some time to achieve, but by the 1750s most Church of Scotland parishes had a school of some sort attached to the church, which was fine so long as the population all belonged to the national church and were distributed in the same way as its churches. The growth of the Secession Church was one blow to the national church's ability to provide education; the 1843 Free Church split was another.

Irish Catholic immigrants provided their own schools, which often doubled as church buildings. Like the Presbyterian schools, they found it difficult to keep pace with the expansion of population and with the demand for children to be educated beyond the rudiments. Although some of those who opposed Popery also objected to Popish schooling, many Protestants were sympathetic to the struggle of Catholic communities to educate their children. The Catholic Schools Society was founded in 1817 with the support of Protestant manufacturers and Thomas Chalmers, the founder of the church in which Begg was a luminary, preached to raise money for RC schools.[53]

Through the nineteenth century the government increasingly became involved in shaping and funding what was becoming a national system of education. The main difference between Church of Scotland schools and those provided by the Catholic Church and dissenting Protestants was not the extent of direct grant aid from the state. Despite vociferous anti-Catholic campaigns, grant aid was given to Catholic as well as to Free Church schools. The main disadvantage was in what might be thought of as local rates. Parishes of the Church in Scotland were originally funded by 'teinds', a local land tax. During the eighteenth and nineteenth centuries, as new congregations were created, this source of revenue declined in relative importance and, of course, it was not available to the various dissenting Presbyterian churches. But it remained an advantage. So that this is not misunderstood as a specifically anti-Catholic policy, we should note that such public funding for the national church was commonplace throughout Europe: until very recently the Scandinavian Lutheran churches were funded by a payroll tax. For Scotland as a whole in 1864 direct state aid accounted for only 15 per cent of the funding for schools and the churches raised another 10 per cent. The majority of funding came from rates (21 per cent), fees (33 per cent) and subscriptions and gifts (20 per cent). It was the 21 per cent in rates that made the great difference between Church of Scotland schools and the rest. And of course the reliance on fees and gifts meant that schools reflected the prosperity (or otherwise) of the families and neighbourhoods that provided their pupils.

In his survey, Handley concludes: 'In the quarter of a century that had elapsed from the enactment of 1847 the state had dealt with the managers and teachers of Catholic schools in a spirit of fairness'.[54] But the need was great. The Argyll Commission of the late 1860s reported that only one-third of Catholic children in Glasgow attended a school of any kind. Attendance itself was irregular because pupils were kept off school for casual labour and most left school at the earliest opportunity anyway. The schools offered very little. As Gallagher notes, 'Catholic education was very rudimentary, school buildings were of inferior standard, and the meagre resources at hand were barely able to provide the three "R's" and religious instruction to a minority of children.'[55]

The 1872 Education Act was the state's response to the failure of a church-based system to serve the needs of a modern industrial urban country whose population was divided between four major churches. A popularly elected school board was to be established in every parish and burgh. It would have the power to manage those schools transferred to it. It would also be able to create new schools, to levy rates to pay for the erection and maintenance of those schools, and to enforce attendance of all children aged between 5 and 13. Religious education was not compulsory but was left to the new boards. However, it was clearly specified that parents could withdraw their children from any religious education of which they disapproved and, to make that easy, such religious education as did take place should occur at the start or the end of the day. With hindsight we can see this as the start of a secular system, but the Presbyterian churches handed over their schools willingly because they simply took it for granted that the popularity of Presbyterianism would be reflected in the composition of local school boards, which in turn would preserve the ethos of the schools. They never anticipated that the local sentiment would eventually become thoroughly secular.

Brown talks of 'the exclusion of Catholic schools from the state system',[56] but this places the decision to stay out of the 1872 settlement in the wrong quarter. Civil servants were anxious to incorporate Catholic schools, but the Catholic Church rejected the terms under which schools could remain denominational: they would have to separate religious instruction from secular teaching. According to James Treble, 'board [that is, state] schools were seen as either an instrument for advancing the interests of the Church of Scotland or, at worst, a force promoting apathy and leading ultimately to the possibility of secularism dominating National Education'.[57]

State support for Catholic schools did not end in 1872. Lay Catholics argued successfully that their schools should continue to be supported from parliamentary grants and local rates; after all, the community was having to contribute to the education of non-Catholic children via the rates that they paid. However, while boards could borrow money on easy terms, the Catholic Church had to rely on its own resources; aid for the maintenance of Catholic schools was awarded only after they had been built and equipped. The consequence of rejecting the 1872 settlement was that Catholic schools failed to improve at the rate of state schools. In 1886, when 71 per cent of female staff employed by the boards had been educated in a training college, the comparable figure for Catholic schools was only 41 per cent.[58] By the end of the First World War, it was becoming clear that the gap in efficiency between Catholic and non-denominational schools was widening, with less than 3 per cent of the Catholic school population receiving secondary education and a shortage of well-qualified teachers.[59] The financial burden was so heavy that the Catholic school system could no longer survive without participating in the public sphere and securing the benefits of local education rates.

Catholic schools were transferred into the state system under the terms of Section 18 of the 1918 Education Act. They were transferred on the understanding that certain safeguards were met: the Church had the right to veto teaching appointments, religious instruction was to carry on to the same degree as before, and Catholic clergymen were to be allowed full access to the schools to oversee the continuation of such mandatory instruction. The schools were actually transferred in 1928, after a 'loan' spell that gave the Catholic authorities the opportunity to see that their demands were being met. The burden for financing and maintaining the schools was removed and, as Gallagher notes, 'in no other predominantly Protestant country did Catholics enjoy such latitude in the educational sphere'.[60]

In fact, the Catholic Church secured a much better deal than did the Free Church of Scotland, which had also built its schools through voluntary contributions but received no safeguards when it handed over control in 1872. Catholic schools have enjoyed both financial security and autonomy in recruitment ever since.

For Catholic teachers, the transfer meant higher salaries and greater security; it was an important boost to the growth of a Catholic middle class. However, the growth of Catholic education was slow for a variety of reasons: the uneven distribution of Catholics across the country, a decline in birth rates, the migration of Catholics out of West Central Scotland, internal shifts in city populations because of redevelopment, government cutbacks during the 1920s and 1930s, and the outbreak of the Second World War.[61] But, even with improved funding, there was one particular weakness of Catholic schooling that should be mentioned because it might go some way to explaining why Catholics were later under-represented in some occupations. Because they had little acquaintance with industrial engineering in Ireland, because they valued highly the scholarship and studiousness of the priest, and because they were often taught by the clergy and by members of teaching orders, the Irish Catholic model of the benefits of education stressed bookishness and academic learning. There was no Catholic equivalent of Allan Glen's: established in 1853 by Glasgow businessmen to promote scientific, technical and craft education. Those Catholic teachers who were not members of religious orders were recruited from secondary schools where the curriculum had been essentially academic. Neither St Mungo's Academy nor St Aloysius College had departments of technical or commercial education and there was thus no great flow of people qualified to teach in these areas. Furthermore, there was not a large pool of experienced skilled

Catholic engineers from which a teaching force may have been drawn.[62] Thus the legacy of Catholic absence from technical occupations from the 1860s kept future generations of Catholics at an educational disadvantage.

Despite its apparently advantageous terms, the 1918 legislation was implemented with very little difficulty. The only significant dispute arose with the Stirlingshire Education Authority. The authority declined to accept responsibility for a new Catholic school in Bonnybridge that had been built against the wishes of the authority, which believed there was already sufficient provision. The case eventually found its way to the House of Lords, which found in favour of the Church.

School board elections encouraged anti-Catholic activists. All the churches fielded slates of candidate. There were varieties of socialists and conservatives (who called themselves 'independents'). And there was the militant Protestant candidate. For many years in Glasgow it was Harry Alfred Long, who was elected to the first board in 1873 as an 'Orange and Protestant Missionary' with 108,264 votes. This sounds like astonishing popularity, but the elections were unusual in that every elector had fifteen votes and could use them all for the same candidate! Long had 3,337 'plumpers', as they were known, and his remaining votes came at an average of 5.2 per person who voted for him. Hence his total support was 14,500 people.[63]

Long was succeeded by the Revd James M. Brisby – an Ulsterman who pastored an independent congregation. In 1911 Brisby came second to the liberal United Free Church (UFC) minister (and socialist) James Barr. We can take his election as proof that the governing structure for education, based as it was on vested interests, polarised the electorate. However, as significant is what happened within the board. At the first meeting after the election, Brisby moved the notion that, because the Protestant voice was not represented on the Voluntary Schools Committee (which dealt with Catholic and Episcopalian schools), no representative of voluntary schools should be permitted to act as convenor or vice-convenor of any other committee. Despite the presence of at least nine Presbyterian clergy, Brisby's motion found no seconder.

We will return to this, but it is instructive to note that radicals may be tamed by institutions and responsibility. Once on the Education Authority and charged with solving practical problems, Harry Long became increasingly moderate and developed good working relations with the priests on the board; Brisby's fate was similar.

Conclusion

There are two general dangers in reading the history of a group of people: supposing they were all alike and supposing that everyone else was different. It is certainly possible to read Handley and suppose that almost all the Irish were poor navvies and coal miners and all the native Scots were not. When reading of the dreadful conditions of the Irish working in the mills, we should remember that exactly these same conditions obtained for Scottish and English mill-workers. The early immigrants were concentrated in unskilled and semi-skilled jobs (which they shared with many Scots) and one reason is clear from an interesting statistic. According to Brown, in 1871 almost half of Catholic brides and grooms (compared to about 11 per cent of members of Protestant churches) were unable to sign the marriage register.[64] The problem with poverty, irrespective of the religion of the poor, is that it is self-reinforcing. As John Treble notes, the poor needed their children to be earning as quickly as possible. Hence their children tended 'to leave school at the earliest opportunity, invariably securing their first jobs in areas where there was no chance of rising socially and economically in adult life'.[65] But Brown adds: 'it would be wrong to regard the Irish Catholic community as uniformly poor.' Many Catholics were able to afford substantial pew rents for their seats in church. There were already in the 1870s Catholic shopkeepers, publicans, pawnbrokers, eating-house owners, schoolteachers, clergymen and solicitors. These could flourish because the Irish Catholic community required servicing, but Catholic businesses did extend beyond the faithful of the parish.

One small detail of the occupations of the second and third generation is worth noting. Handley mentions the police.[66] One of the marks of deep social division in Northern Ireland since its formation in 1921 is the refusal of Catholic nationalists to accept the legitimacy of the state. At partition, many Royal Irish Constabulary officers in the north-east accepted a transfer to what became the Irish Free State. Thereafter Catholic enrolment tailed off and during the Troubles it almost ended altogether. There has never been any such unwillingness to serve the state among the Irish Catholic immigrants to Scotland.

Although not alienated to the same extent as their Belfast counterparts, Catholics were clearly demarcated by their shared religion,
which was sustained not just by the Church but also by an array of
ancillary organisations. The Society of St Vincent de Paul provided
social welfare. The Catholic Young Men's Society provided church-
approved social activities. Football clubs (see Chapter 4) provided
sporting activities and a focus for joint celebration of a shared
identity. The League of the Cross provided a network of games
rooms to serve as an alternative to the public house. And the schools
provided a vehicle for monitoring and controlling families. Handley
describes the Catholic parish of the late nineteenth century as

> a self-contained unit . . . in the work and leisure of that body the
> local teachers played an important role. They were called upon to
> organise all sorts of parish activities, from winter concerts to mid-
> summer excursions. The strong link that bound school to church
> was largely of their forging. Parents and grandparents whom they
> had taught turned to them for advice in their difficulties.[67]

As Gallagher puts it: 'The Irish side of the ghetto frontier may even
have been patrolled more vigorously from the inside than the
outside.'[68]

However, that picture needs some amendment. Bernard Aspinwall, the most productive of modern historians of the Catholic
Church in Scotland, warns against the myth of the homogenous
poor faithful community. He notes that 'vicious internecine struggles
between Irish- and Scottish-born Catholic clergy and laity alike
reached depths that make contemporary anti-Catholic virulence
seem tame by comparison'.[69] He also notes the role of wealthy
Catholic families in bankrolling:

> religious orders of men and women, churches, schools, teachers,
> choirmasters and the rest. The churches they scattered across the
> land are astonishing in number – an inconvenient fact for those
> believers in 'the pennies of the [Irish] poor only' version of
> Scottish Catholicism.

These qualifications remind us of a point made at the start of the
chapter. Not all the Irish migrants were Catholics and not all
Catholics are descended from Irish migrants. But, even if they
had been similar in circumstance, there would have been enough

variation in individual choices to make us cautious of talking of a 'community', let alone a 'ghetto'.

We do not underestimate anti-Catholic bigotry, but we do draw attention to a neglected feature of that bigotry: far from representing the power of militant Protestantism, as often as not it grew from impotence and marginality. We have also questioned the conventional history that takes discrimination as its master theme. The historical record provides far less clear evidence of discrimination than the routine repetition of a few sources would suggest. We also point to an important but neglected consideration. It is obviously very difficult to do this in retrospect, but we must distinguish between the obstacles to upward mobility that resulted from characteristics of the migrant population and the barriers that were placed in the way of such mobility by those who wished to see Irish Catholics remain poor. Even if all the migrants had been of the same religion as the native Scots, most immigrant families would still have started their lives in Scotland at the bottom of the labour market, and the lack of capital and industrial skills would have retarded upward social mobility for a number of generations.

Notes

1. In an interesting example of how partisan myths are created, this process is described by Burdsey and Chappell as 'Catholics were forced into the peripheral regions of Scotland'. The new ideas spread in a certain pattern. No people were forced anywhere. D. Burdsey and R. Chappell, '"and if you know your history": An examination of the formation of football clubs in Scotland and their role in the construction of social identity', *Sports Historian*, 21 (May 2001); http://www2.umist.ac.uk/sport/SPORTS%HISTORY/sh211.html

2. For those unfamiliar with church history, 'Episcopalian' in this context denotes the 'semi-Reformed' nature of the state Church of England since Henry VIII: largely Protestant in core doctrines and independent of Rome but retaining the hierarchical structure of archbishop and bishops and some of the ritual elements of the Roman Church. For brief periods, the English model was imposed on Scotland and hence remnants of Episcopalianism remained. In the twentieth century the Scottish Episcopal Church was regularly topped up by English settlers.

3. R. H. Campbell, *Scotland since 1707* (Oxford: Basil Blackwell, 1965).

4. J. Hunter, *The Making of the Crofting Community* (Edinburgh: John Donald, 1978).

5. Sir David Stewart of Garth, *Sketches of the Character, Manners and Present State of the Highlanders of Scotland etc.* (Edinburgh: Archibald Constable, 1822), p. 57.

6. Hunter, *Crofting Community*, p. 101.

7. J. Kennedy, *The Days of the Fathers in Ross-shire* (Inverness: Christian Focus Publications, 1979), p. 29.

8. The Seceders were evangelical Presbyterians who objected to the right of heritors (usually the major landowners) to select ministers. Various strands of Seceder Presbyterianism eventually amalgamated as the United Presbyterian Church.

9. C. A. Pigott, 'A Geography of Religion in Scotland' (Edinburgh University: Ph.D. thesis, 1979), p. 63.

10. These figures come from J. E. Handley, *The Irish in Scotland* (Glasgow: Burns, 1964); a collation of his *The Irish in Scotland* and *The Irish in Modern Scotland* published by Cork University Press in 1945 and 1947 respectively.

11. J. Devine, 'A Lanarkshire perspective on bigotry in Scottish society', in T. Devine (ed.), *Scotland's Shame? Bigotry and Sectarianism in Modern Scotland* (Edinburgh: Mainstream, 2000), p. 101.

12. G. Walker, *Intimate Strangers: Political and Cultural Interaction between Scotland and Ulster in Modern Times* (Edinburgh: John Donald, 1995), p. 8.

13. For excellent histories of Orangeism in Scotland, see W. S. Marshall, *The Billy Boys: A Concise History of Orangeism in Scotland* (Edinburgh: Mercat Press, 1996) and E. McFarland, *Protestants First: Orangeism in 19th Century Scotland* (Edinburgh: Edinburgh University Press, 1990).

14. C. G. Brown, *The Social History of Religion in Scotland since 1730* (London: Methuen, 1987), p. 164.

15. Walker, *Intimate Strangers,* p. 9.

16. Handley, *The Irish in Scotland*, p. 273.

17. A. B. Campbell, *The Lanarkshire Miners 1775–1874* (Edinburgh: John Donald, 1979), pp. 193–5, 223.

18. J. H. Treble, 'The market for unskilled male labour in Glasgow, 1891–1914', in I. MacDougall (ed.), *Essays in Scottish Labour History* (Edinburgh: John Donald, 1978), p. 121.

19. On Orange lodges in the coalfields, see Marshall, *The Billy Boys*.

20. Campbell, *The Lanarkshire Miners*; see also M. Mitchell, *The Irish in the West of Scotland 1979–1848: Trade Unions, Strikes and Political Movements* (Edinburgh: John Donald, 1998).

21. A. L. Drummond and J. Bulloch, *The Church in Victorian Scotland, 1843–1874* (Edinburgh: Saint Andrew Press, 1975), pp. 70–4.

22. T. Gallagher, *Glasgow: The Uneasy Peace* (Manchester: Manchester University Press, 1987), p.12.

23. Brown, *Social History of Religion*, p. 33.

24. E. H. Hunt, *British Labour History 1815–1914* (London: Weidenfeld and Nicolson, 1981), p. 162.

25. I. A. Muirhead, 'Catholic emancipation: Scottish reactions in 1829', *Innes Review*, 24 (1973), pp. 26–42.

26. W. Hanna, *Memoirs of the Life and Writing of Thomas Chalmers*, vol. III (Edinburgh: Thomas Constable, 1892), p. 239.

27. Thomas Smith, *Memoirs of Revd James Begg* (Edinburgh: John Gemmell, 1885), p. 70

28. Ibid. pp. 133–5.
29. Wylie was a permanent lecturer of the Protestant Institute, set up by the SRS in 1860.
30. J. A. Wylie, *Disruption Worthies: A Memorial of 1843* (Edinburgh: T. C. Jack, 1881).
31. D. Jamie, *John Hope, Philanthropist & Reformer* (Edinburgh: Hope Trust, 1907), p. 119.
32. Ibid. p. 131.
33. Ibid. p. 251.
34. J. B. Primmer, *The Life of Jacob Primmer: Minister of the Church of Scotland* (Edinburgh: William Bishop, 1916).
35. Ibid. p. 60.
36. Ibid. p. 88.
37. Handley, *The Irish in Scotland*, p. 242.
38. Gallagher, *Glasgow*, p. 19.
39. For those unfamiliar with the theological implications of this and who might otherwise read it as Protestants merely being awkward for the sake of it, there was an important issue at stake for those who believed in such things. The Catholic Church did not see itself as one of a number of equally valid expressions of Christianity. Rather it was the true church and in its mind the creation of a provincial structure was the restoration of the Christian Church, which had been in abeyance since Henry had rejected the authority of Rome. Especially for the Church of England, which regarded itself as the continuing embodiment of Christ's gospel, the restoration of the Catholic hierarchy was a major insult to the legitimacy of Protestantism.
40. Handley, *The Irish in Scotland*, p. 236.
41. Gallagher, *Glasgow*, p. 22.
42. D. McRaild, *Culture, Conflict and Migration: The Irish in Victorian Cumbria* (Liverpool: Liverpool University Press, 1998). Marshall (*The Billy Boys*, p. 33) mentions that a Twelfth procession in Dundee in 1847 was attacked by a hostile mob of Irish Catholics.
43. W. L. Arnstein, 'The Murphy riots: a Victorian dilemma', *Victorian Studies*, 19 (1975), pp. 51–71.
44. Quoted in Handley, *The Irish in Scotland*, p. 108.
45. Ibid. p. 310.
46. Ibid. p. 251.
47. Ibid. p. 251. The tolerant attitudes displayed by *The Scotsman* could be explained by the fact that for thirty years from 1876 the editor was an English Catholic: Charles Cooper. However, that they were mirrored by the *Glasgow Herald* suggests that the elite preference for social order was a greater consideration.
48. Handley, *The Irish in Scotland*, p. 278.
49. J. Cooney, *Scotland and the Papacy: Pope John Paul II's Visit in Perspective* (Edinburgh: Paul Harris, 1982), p. 36.
50. Handley, *The Irish in Scotland*, p. 259.
51. Ibid. p. 260. It is worth adding that the restoration of the hierarchy in Scotland

caused little public clamour. The most excited opposition came from the small Episcopalian Church, which insisted that it was already the rightful occupant of the ancient sees of the Christian Church in Scotland.

52. Gallagher, *Glasgow*, p. 29.
53. A. L. Drummond and J. Bulloch, *The Scottish Church 1688–1843* (Edinburgh: Saint Andrew Press, 1973), p. 141.
54. Handley, *The Irish in Scotland*, p. 311.
55. Gallagher, *Glasgow*, p.57.
56. Brown, *Social History of Religion*, p. 164.
57. J. H. Treble, 'The development of Roman Catholic education in Scotland 1878–1978', in D. McRoberts (ed.), *Modern Scottish Catholicism* (Glasgow: Burns, 1979), p. 111.
58. L. Paterson, *Scottish Education in the Twentieth Century* (Edinburgh: Edinburgh University Press, 2003), p. 40.
59. T. A. Fitzpatrick, *Catholic Secondary Education in South-West Scotland before 1872* (Aberdeen: Aberdeen University Press, 1986), p. 34
60. Gallagher, *Glasgow*, p.103. We should add that in the early years of the system Scots who were not supporters of the Catholic Church could feel aggrieved that public funds were directly subsidising the Church because staff who were members of Catholic teaching orders often gave part of their salary to the Church.
61. Treble, 'Roman Catholic education', pp. 123–4.
62. Fitzpatrick, *Catholic Secondary Education*, p. 80.
63. Parliamentary Accounts and Papers, 1873: Volume LII: Ecclesiastical; Education, Science and Art [412], Return showing the Number of School Boards Elected in Scotland.
64. Brown, *Social History of Religion*, p. 151.
65. Treble, 'Roman Catholic education', p. 125.
66. Handley, *The Irish in Scotland*, p. 272.
67. Ibid. p. 317.
68. Gallagher, *Glasgow*, p. 19.
69. B. Aspinwall, 'Faith of our fathers living still . . . The time warp or Woof! Woof!', in T. Devine (ed.), *Scotland's Shame? Bigotry and Sectarianism in Modern Scotland* (Edinburgh: Mainstream, 2000), p. 110.

2 The Thirties

Introduction

The period between the two world wars was crucial in the history of sectarianism. Though it came back to haunt Britain fifty years later, the Irish problem was resolved enough for the Irish in Britain to shift their political interests from Home Rule to local issues. As immigration slowed to a trickle, the proportion of Catholics born in Scotland grew steadily. Organized labour came to power in many local councils and the first Labour government took office in Westminster. The relative decline of the Presbyterian churches became apparent. The brief period of post-1918 prosperity gave way to deep depression. It was in this context that the new Scots and the old Scots had to decide their future.

Home Rule and Electoral Politics

To make sense of the political developments of the 1930s we need to backtrack a little. Late nineteenth-century Catholic politics in Glasgow operated at two, rather separate, levels. School board democracy meant elections and the Catholic Union (established during the 1885 education election campaign) channelled the Catholic vote for school boards and other local Catholic interests.

At the Westminster level politics were concerned with Irish home rule.

> The Irish vote . . . was a solid and highly disciplined one which the branches delivered according to the instructions of the head of the Irish Parliamentary party, who was not concerned with British domestic issues, but with completing Ireland's national struggle.[1]

The 1886 Home Rule Bill had started a process that was fundamentally to alter Scottish politics. It ended fifty years of Liberal domination in Scotland by splitting the Liberals into Home Rulers and Unionists.

The various extensions of the franchise and the growing pressure from Ireland for independence created the first home-rule crisis of the 1880s and the conflict had considerable impact on the political life of western Scotland, as it had on Liverpool and Lancashire, with many Irish Scots being active in Irish political organisations. A number of Scots were actually elected to Westminster as home-rulers by Irish constituencies.[2] The same quarrels in the second decade of the twentieth century had far less impact, perhaps because, as Tom Gallagher argues, while the first crisis coincided with economic depression in Scotland and raised local fears about the influx of poor people that would follow the collapse of the Irish economy, the second coincided with a period of relative prosperity on the Clyde and in the mining valleys of Ayrshire and Lanarkshire.[3]

Scottish support for the Ulster unionist cause was muted. When Sir Edward Carson came to speak in Glasgow, only 8,000 turned out to hear him. In contrast, Liverpool managed to produce over 150,000 people at 7.00 a.m. on a Sunday morning.[4] The Glasgow Presbytery of the Church of Scotland passed a motion condemning home rule but it was left to an independent evangelical minister originally from Ulster, the Revd James McBurney Brisby, to give clerical legitimation to the Scottish branches of the Ulster Volunteer Force (UVF).[5] Despite the close ties between Ulster and Scotland, the Orange Order could raise only seven UVF units, totalling no more than 1,000 men. In Ulster the two main Protestant churches, the Presbyterians and the Episcopalian Church of Ireland, were heavily involved in promoting the signing of the pro-Union Covenant; in Glasgow, the show of solidarity had to be organised by an independent émigré.

The onset of the First World War in 1914 turned attention away from Ireland, but the Sinn Fein rising in Dublin in 1916 provoked a minor revival of anti-Irish sentiment, ably voiced by the character of Andrew Amos, the disillusioned Border radical in John Buchan's *Mr Standfast*, whose description of Ulster perfectly captures the grudging sense of Presbyterian common identity.

> Glasgow's stinkin' nowadays with two things, money and Irish. I mind the day when I followed Mr Gladstone's Home Rule policy, and used to threep about the noble, generous, warm-hearted sister nation held in a foreign bondage. My Goad! I'm not speakin' about Ulster, which is a dour, ill-natured den, but our own folk all the same. But the men that will not do a hand's turn to help the war and take the chance of our necessities to set up a bawbee rebellion are hateful to Goad and man.[6]

As there were far more Irish Catholics than Ulster Protestants in Scotland, it is no surprise that support for Sinn Fein was considerably greater than support for the UVF. Gallagher writes that 'by 1921 almost every Scottish town with a sizeable Irish presence had its own IRA company'.[7] The aftermath of the 1916 rising brought an increase in Irish political activity, with a large number of Sinn Fein branches being founded in the west coast of Scotland and a lot of money being raised for the nationalist cause. But the partition of Ireland and the consolidation of the Free State and Northern Ireland governments allowed the Irish question to slide from the front pages.

It was the genius of John Wheatley and Patrick Dollan to combine the class and Irish impulses within Catholic politics and to direct them towards the emerging labour movement. Wheatley, a successful businessman and committed Catholic, formed the Catholic Socialist Society in 1906, aiming to show that socialism and Catholicism were not incompatible. He was elected to Lanarkshire County Council in 1909 and Glasgow Town Council in 1912. His position was initially uncomfortable; he was denounced by many Glasgow priests and once memorably found himself burnt in effigy outside his front door by an angry Catholic mob, which he managed to talk round.[8] He became a leading figure in the Independent Labour Party (ILP). Patrick Dollan, a former miner turned journalist, supported Wheatley and became a key organiser of the Catholic Union. Wheatley was one of the ILP candidates elected to Westminster in the famous 'Red Clydeside' election of 1922 – a campaign that Dollan had organised. He eventually became a minister in Ramsey Macdonald's government. Dollan was elected to Glasgow Town Council in 1913 and remained until 1946. He was the leader of the Labour group from 1922 until 1938 and then Lord Provost from 1938 to 1941. In that year he was knighted for his services to local government. Although the Catholic bloc Wheatley and Dollan constructed was never as formidable (or as corrupt) as New York's Tammany Hall machine, it was an efficient vehicle for shifting Irish Catholic support from Home Rule to Labour.[9]

In brief, the removal of Ireland from the agenda allowed Glasgow Catholics to focus on domestic politics and for most that meant working through the Labour Party. The decline of the Liberals reconfigured Glasgow politics. The extension of the franchise saw a gradual shift in power to Labour and the strong Catholic presence in that party allowed the descendants of the Irish in the western industrial Lowlands access to considerable power and influence. However, the shift to the left in Scottish politics and the attendant rise of western Catholics were not even or unchallenged. We will now consider four attempts to prevent that process: the short-lived Orange Party, the Church of Scotland's brief flirtation with racism, and the rapid rise and fall of both the Scottish Protestant League and Protestant Action.

Hugh Ferguson: The First and Last No-Popery MP

Hugh Ferguson served as the independent MP for Motherwell and Wishaw for one parliamentary term, over 1923–4. An auctioneer and scrap-metal merchant, Ferguson was an active member of the Plymouth Brethren and the Orange Order. He had long been involved in the politics of Motherwell, a town frequently associated with sectarian friction, serving as an Independent councillor on Lanarkshire council. In the election of 1918 Ferguson opposed the official Unionist nominee as an Independent, but finished a poor fourth behind an Independent Liberal. However, he was to benefit from a temporary rift between the Orange Order and the Unionist hierarchy. The ambition of Scottish Orangeism was to win the kind of role in the Unionist machine enjoyed by their Ulster brethren. It is a mark of the marginality of the Scottish Order that their first, severely limited, success in this regard came only in 1912, when it won the right to two permanent representatives on the Unionist's Western Divisional Council. How little that was worth became clear nine years later when the Order resigned the seats to protest against the decision of the Scottish Unionists to endorse the establishment of the Irish Free State. It then announced a political break with the Unionists and the formation of the Orange and Protestant Party (OPP), although little came of this initiative. The OPP's only election contest was to field two candidates in Motherwell during the 1922 Lanarkshire Education Election: they were the only candidates in the parish not to be elected. In 1922 the Unionists withdrew their Parliamentary candidate from Motherwell in favour of a Liberal, and Ferguson, standing with OPP support, came a good second. Labour won the seat in 1922 largely because the Liberal vote split between a National and a 'Free' Liberal. In 1923 Ferguson captured Motherwell at his third attempt, winning a 1,000-vote majority over the Labour incumbent. Orangeism's 'Protestantism before Politics' faction now had Parliamentary representation, but little good it did. Although he took the Unionist whip, Ferguson proved a figure of ridicule, and was denounced from his own benches as a 'common informer . . . despised by everyone'.[10] Ferguson's single achievement as a parliamentarian was to persuade Lanarkshire's Chief Constable that a Catholic procession in Carfin was in contravention of the 1829 Catholic Emancipation Act. Like every other militant Protestant triumph, that victory turned out to be hollow. The controversy it provoked led more or less directly to the removal of most of the remaining Catholic disabilities through the virtually unopposed 1926 Catholic Relief Act.

By then Ferguson was no longer an MP, and the manner of his defeat is telling. Neither Liberal nor Unionist stood in Motherwell in 1924, leaving the field open for a straight fight between Ferguson and Labour. Labour's choice of candidate was inspired. The Revd James Barr was a leading figure in the United Free Church (UFC). His profession meant that, without playing up religious conflict, he cut away much of Ferguson's appeal. Barr did so well that Mother-well bucked the trend as the only Scottish seat that Labour took from the Unionists in 1924. Ferguson threatened to contest a subsequent Dundee by-election, but the city's Unionists made it clear that he was unwelcome. His attentions briefly switched to education, but he managed only a single term (1925–8) on Lanarkshire Education Authority. His removal from Parliament spelled the end of the half-hearted OPP project, and both it and Ferguson slid into obscurity.

The Kirk's Disgrace: Racialising Catholics

In 2002 the General Assembly of the Church of Scotland officially apologised for the stance taken by some of its leaders eighty years earlier. That campaign began in 1922 against a background of spiralling unemployment, impressive advances by Labour in west central Scotland (in some part aided by the urban Catholic vote), and the establishment of the Irish Free State. The spark for it came from Glasgow, where a small coterie of ministers had used anti-Catholic rhetoric to drum up enthusiasm during elections to the Education Authority. Buoyed by its apparent success, the caucus, led by Revd Duncan Cameron of Kilsyth, placed anti-Catholic and anti-Irish motions before the Church of Scotland's General Assembly. Cameron argued that

> Roman Catholics of Irish origin . . . were not only alien to Scots in religion; they were also alien in race. They had come to Scotland to take jobs from Scottish workers, to exploit Scotland's welfare resources and to stir labour unrest . . . Irish Catholic men were also seducing innocent Scottish girls into mixed marriages 'to betray the faith of their fathers'. The presence of the Irish Catholic aliens, he prophesied, would soon bring racial and sectarian warfare to Scotland.[11]

Many members of the assembly expressed grave doubts as to the wisdom of such attacks, and the matter was remitted for further consideration only on the deciding vote of the Moderator. The following year the Church and Nation Committee submitted its report, chillingly entitled *The Menace of the Irish Race to our Scottish Nationality*. The report argued of Irish Catholic migrants and their descendants:

> They cannot be assimilated and absorbed into the Scottish race. They remain a people by themselves, segregated by reason of their race, their customs, their traditions and above all by their loyalty

to their Church, and are gradually and inevitably dividing Scotland, racially, socially and ecclesiastically.[12]

The report highlighted a number of religious themes (such as the state funding of Catholic schools; the Church's attitude to mixed marriages; and Vatican 'scheming'), but its main thrust was that countries divided on racial lines could never prosper. Indeed, dire consequences were predicted:

> Already there is a bitter feeling among the Scottish working classes against the Irish intruders. As the latter increases, and the Scottish people realise the seriousness of the menace to their own racial supremacy in their native land, this bitterness will develop into a race antagonism which will have disastrous consequences for Scotland.[13]

Yet the report blurred these racial lines by insisting that the Orange Irish, 'loyal' and Protestant, were exempted from criticism.

This appeal to race marked a radical break with previous Presbyterian complaints about Scotland's Catholics. In part this reflected the feeling that issues of race (which today we would call 'national' or 'ethnic') were scientific and respectable whereas appeals to religious difference were not. Certainly the campaign quickly set out to deny any notion of religious antagonism. In 1923 the Kirk appointed Revd John White, a key champion of Presbyterian union, to lead the anti-Irish campaign. This appointment (and the campaign itself) can be understood only against a background of the delicate union negotiations between the Kirk and the UFC. Because being Scottish and being Protestant were two things that all sections of both churches had in common, united action against the 'Irish menace' was seen by some as a way of encouraging a sense of shared identity and thus smoothing the remaining obstacles to union. White took great pains to dissociate the campaign from 'petty' sectarianism, assuring the 1927 General Assembly:

> They dealt with this very difficult, delicate, and important question entirely from the racial point of view. The religious factor did not enter the question at all . . . Uncontrolled immigration was always a menace to a community, especially if it was to continue alongside the emigration of young and energetic native-born citizens.[14]

This latter point was of widespread concern. Between 1919 and 1926 about 300,000 Scots emigrated. Many of them were migrants from Ireland, but this did not soften Scots' fears about the fate of their own race. George Malcolm Thomson's *Caledonia* announced grimly: 'The Scots are a dying people.'[15] John Buchan, a respected politician and author not known for intemperance, said in a 1932 parliamentary debate:

> something must be done, and done soon if Scotland is not to lose its historic individuality. All is not well with our country. Our population is declining; we are losing some of the best of our race stock by migration and their place is being taken by those who, whatever their merits, are not Scottish. I understand that every fifth child born in Scotland is an Irish Roman Catholic.[16]

In 1928 the churchmen finally won an opportunity to present their case to the Conservative government: a delegation was granted less than an hour with William Joynson-Hicks, the Home Secretary, and Scottish Secretary Sir John Gilmour. The delegates were to receive a rude shock. To mollify them, they were promised 'the fullest inquiry' into the legal position of recent Irish migrants who became destitute, but they were also handed government data that flatly contradicted their case. With what must have required a considerable amount of self-control for a Unionist MP and member of the Orange Order's Grand Lodge, Gilmour told the petitioners that, even if it had been the problem they asserted, migration from the Irish Free State could not be prevented because it was not a foreign country: it was part of the British Empire!

In 1929 the *Glasgow Herald* challenged the evidential basis for the campaign. In a series of articles the paper 'demonstrated what was already obvious': that economic recession had reduced Irish immigration into Scotland to 'a mere trickle', and that the Irish-born were under-represented amongst poor-relief claimants. The *Glasgow Herald* concluded that the Presbyterian case could 'no longer be effectively pressed'.[17] A further blow came with the census of 1931, which showed that the numbers of Irish-born, far from increasing, had declined sharply over the 1920s. Further, a majority of the Irish-born were from Northern Ireland, further discrediting Presbyterian claims about the rising number of migrants from the Irish Free State.

After seven years the Presbyterian case had ground to a halt. The Conservative government had simply ignored requests for a hearing until they had acquired the statistical basis to reject the Presbyterian case. All the more galling was the fact that the delegation had expected Gilmour, an active Orangeman, to be sympathetic. He was not and nor was his successor. William Adamson, an evangelical Baptist, became Secretary of State for Scotland in the Labour government. When, in May 1930, White led another delegation, Adamson dismissed his schemes out of hand.

With the legislative path closed to them, the campaigners changed tack. The 1930 General Assembly decided to appeal 'to the patriotism of their Scottish labour employers' to instigate an economic barrier against 'Irish' labour.[18] The new strategy quickly flopped. In 1930 a senior Churchman alleged that Catholic Irish foremen at Peterhead harbour works were discriminating in favour of their countrymen. The subsequent government investigation found that no Irish foremen were employed at the works, and, of the workforce of 370, just two men had been born in Ireland.[19] By the mid-1930s the campaign was without credibility, and a heated debate at the 1935 General Assembly effectively killed it off. One minister asked:

> Was it worthy of the Church of Scotland, at a time when materialism was rampant and sheer paganism not only beyond the Rhine but in their own midst, that they should engage in that agitation against a Church which, however they deplored her errors, did stand for spiritual things, and on the side of Christ?[20]

In its immediate political aims the campaign was an abject failure. It did not produce restrictions on Irish Free State immigration or a revision of the 1918 Education Act. But its greater failure lay in its underlying and implicit aims to reassert Presbyterian authority by scapegoating the Catholic Irish minority. No attempt was made to win over public opinion, as the campaigners believed they could make a persuasive case without a public campaign. The arrogant belief that the Kirk, in particular after Presbyterian reunion, spoke for Scotland and could expect the government to listen, was simply mistaken. Successive governments – Conservative, Labour and National – did not listen, and indeed scorned the campaign. Senior Scottish Unionists, including those like Gilmour who might, on the surface, have been expected to support White, steered clear. Both elite daily newspapers in Scotland – Edinburgh's *Scotsman* and the *Glasgow Herald* – were cool towards the campaign, with the *Herald* by 1929 profoundly and influentially critical.

Neither did the campaign capture the mood of Scotland's intellectuals. Two prominent right-wing Scottish nationalists did align themselves with the tenor (if not the practicalities) of the campaign. George Malcolm Thomson predicted that Scotland would be Catholic by the late twentieth century,[21] and argued that the Kirk's campaign lacked substance and revealed 'callous indifference' to the Irish menace: 'the public spirit of the Church is suspect. They think of congregation rather than nation.'[22] Andrew Dewar Gibb argued that, without the Irish, Scotland 'would be the most law abiding country in the world': 'Wheresoever knives and razors are used, wheresoever sneak thefts and petty pilfering are easy and safe, wheresoever dirty acts of sexual baseness are committed, there you will find the Irishman in Scotland with all but a monopoly of the business.'[23] However, this was unrepresentative of literary Scotland between the wars. Christopher Grieve (Hugh McDiarmid) welcomed Irish immigration as strengthening Scotland's Celtic identity and such well-known figures of the literary renaissance as Edwin Muir, Lewis Grassic Gibbon and William Power viewed the declining power of the Kirk with glee. Compton Mackenzie, popular novelist and Catholic, went further, insisting that 'Satan himself . . . can fairly be regarded as the first Protestant of all'.[24]

The campaign against the Irish, therefore, had only limited political support. Those people within Unionism who liked it lacked influence. Unionists with influence did not like it.[25] And, whilst a small number of intellectuals were prepared to dabble in the murky waters of anti-Irishness, many more found deeply disturbing the Kirk's attempt to reassert its social and political authority in this manner. It is worth noting that by the mid-1950s, when Augustus Muir wrote his biography of John White, anti-Catholicism had become so outdated that Muir does not even mention once a theme that had been a major part of White's working life.[26]

The campaign did find favour exactly where it might be expected: on the militant Protestant fringe. An important, if entirely unintended, consequence of the campaign was to grant to this fringe a veneer of ecclesiastical sanction they had not enjoyed for a century. These bodies, however, were suspicious both of the motivations of career churchmen like White and of the half-hearted support the campaign enjoyed in many sections of the Kirk. The Scottish Reformation Society (SRS), for example, complained of: 'a refusal to look at the growing menace which Rome brings to a community. It is not easy to persuade some people that we are simply taking our stand as upholders of the Reformation, and . . . of religious and political liberty.'[27] The active opposition of the political mainstream to the campaign allowed fringe Protestant political figures to lay claim to policies proposed by Scotland's mainstream Protestant churches. Unable to persuade respectable parties of the justice of their campaign, the churches faced the unpleasant fact that their calls were answered by populist demagogues with whom they were loathe to be associated. Ironically it was the unwelcome political successes of militants in the mid-1930s that persuaded most Kirk ministers that the campaign had been a mistake. It is to the political entrepreneurs of anti-Catholicism – and their failure to garner and hold public support – that we now turn.

Alexander Ratcliffe and the Scottish Protestant League

The brief parliamentary career of Ferguson suggests that militant Protestantism was marginal to Scottish political life. The career of Leith railway clerk and lay preacher Alexander Ratcliffe (1888–1947) confirms it. Ratcliffe was a follower of Jacob Primmer, who billed his Scottish Protestant League (SPL), founded in 1920, as a 'new aggressive Protestant movement' that intended to oppose 'spiritualism, Christian Science, and various other systems of anti-Scriptural teaching [as well as] Roman Catholic Sinn Fein'.[28] Despite this broad remit, the SPL was almost exclusively concerned with No Popery themes: the evils of the confessional, convent horror stories and escapes, the power and secrecy of the Jesuits and priestly immorality. In 1925 Ratcliffe manufactured a localised controversy over Catholic schools, on the back of which he was elected to the Edinburgh Education Authority. The victory was a shallow one. Despite assembling a fairly creditable slate of candidates, including a parish councillor and a Free Church theologian, Ratcliffe was elected by the very narrowest of margins and his colleagues polled abysmally. His tenure on the authority was unhappy and unproductive; not even Church of Scotland clergymen who were members of the

Orange Order supported him. There were brief glimpses of influence. In 1928, for example, the SPL was able to mount a public lecture in Perth City Hall with Duncan Cameron, one of the early instigators of the Presbyterian anti-Irish campaign, as the main speaker and Lord Scone, a young Unionist who subsequently became Honorary President of the SPL, in the chair. But by the end of the decade Ratcliffe had little to show for his efforts. His impact on educational politics had been nil. The electoral alliance he had cobbled together in 1925 did not survive that election; and his core support base was limited to a tiny militant Protestant fringe. Scone apart, the League had no major public figures willing to be associated with it and SPL activities amounted to little more than producing its newspaper and the occasional controversial lecture. This last activity could be lucrative – hundreds paid to hear Edith O'Gorman, the 'escaped nun', and Monica Farrell, 'converted Roman Catholic', recount their adventures – but it was not going to shift Scottish opinion.

The 1929 general election offered Ratcliffe a new platform, and he chose to contest Falkirk and Stirling Burghs, where the defending Labour MP, Hugh Murnin, was Catholic, and the Unionist nominee, Douglas Jamieson, had strong Orange connections. The constituency was also home to an unresolved legal wrangle between the Catholic Church and Stirlingshire Education Authority. By emphasising this issue and Murnin's Catholicism Ratcliffe tried to embarrass Jamieson into endorsing a policy of repealing the 1918 Education Act, and of restricting Catholic Irish immigration. Jamieson dismissed Ratcliffe's suggestions and lost the election by 5,000 votes, Ratcliffe picking up an impressive 7,000. It is thus possible that Jamieson could have taken the seat had he acceded to Ratcliffe's demands, but Ratcliffe's offer to withdraw was impossible for any Unionist to accept. Jamieson represented a party that had broader interests in both British and Scottish terms. English Conservatives were staunch supporters of Anglican schools, and it was thus difficult for any Unionist to build a platform around principled opposition to denominational education. The wider Scottish interest was the long courtship of erstwhile Liberal voters. Unionists were loathe to play anything more controversial that the anti-Socialist card.

Ratcliffe learned several key lessons in 1929: his message had electoral appeal given the correct set of circumstances but it depended on him competing with a Unionist Party he had hitherto tried to court. To maximise his appeal he had to burn those few bridges to respectable Protestantism he had struggled to build. Lord Scone, furious that the SPL had entered the lists against a fellow Unionist, publicly broke with Ratcliffe. Given that Scone was locked in a North Lanark contest where the Labour candidate was under Catholic pressure over her views on birth control, it seems that he had come to realise the potential costs of playing the Protestant card.

During 1930 Ratcliffe moved the League to Glasgow, where it quickly gained momentum. Three candidates entered the 1931 municipal election and against expectations took one safe Moderate (as the Conservative-led anti-socialist alliance was known) and one safe Labour ward. Ratcliffe took Dennistoun from the Moderates, while Charlie Forrester, a former Communist, took Dalmarnock. The SPL entered politics at a time of great ideological flux, with the right deeply discredited, and the left deeply divided. After taking another seat in 1932, the SPL peaked in 1933, taking four seats and 68,000 votes, which was 22 per cent of the poll. Yet from here the League disintegrated, as Ratcliffe's autocratic style alienated his supporters: all seven seats, including Ratcliffe's, were lost at their first defence.

That was the end of electoral Protestantism in Glasgow: the SPL stood no candidates in 1935 and in 1937 Ratcliffe polled weakly in Camphill ward. The League had burst into Glasgow politics like a firework: an impressive explosion that burnt out and left a handful of cinders falling to earth. Its major consequence was to weaken the ability of the right to resist the rise of Labour. Patrick Dollan took control of Glasgow in 1933, thanks in no small part to the four wards taken by the SPL, and the Labour Party has ruled it almost unin- terrupted since.

The League's appeal rested on a complex mix of grievance and fear amongst many sections of the Glasgow electorate. The middle classes were furious that the Moderate alliance had failed to keep their rates low, whilst the working classes were suffering under the austerity measures adopted in 1931. Unemployment was rising steadily, and with it the cost of 'the dole' on the public purse. Stringent curbs on public assistance spawned militant protests by the unemployed: the Lord Provost's effigy was burned in St Enoch

Square, and several days later a huge protest demonstration of the unemployed was broken up by police, leading to serious rioting and the arrest of ILP leaders. This left the ruling Moderates charged with callous indifference, and the left tainted with the damage and chaos of the riot. The SPL offered a way out for disillusioned Moderate voters who did not trust the left. Ratcliffe made a specific play for council employees who had been obliged to endure a substantial pay cut. It was not difficult for Ratcliffe to identify two sorts of political space to exploit. The League targeted Dennistoun and Partick East, where the Moderates were split over austerity, and appealed to Labour voters appalled at the recent violence. In these seats, composed of lower middle and skilled working-class voters, Ratcliffe adopted an opportunistic platform, arguing against corruption and waste, against cuts in corporation salaries and for reductions in the council's rent and rates. A very different kind of populism was employed in Dalmarnock, where a notorious Bridgeton gang, the 'Billy Boys', was engaged as muscle in an uproarious and violent campaign. Success at the first outing in Dalmarnock and Dennistoun suggested that both respectable and rough strategies could work.

In 1932, however, Ratcliffe downplayed the respectable populism and targeted Labour's working-class wards, particularly those with a strong Orange subculture. Ratcliffe may have been persuaded that divisions on the political left offered the SPL a chance to win the working-class vote, but results revealed that it was Moderate seats that were most vulnerable to the League: the only SPL victory displaced a sitting Moderate. Although the SPL pushed close in some wards (Labour held Shettleston by just seventy-one votes), the overall lesson was that the SPL was taking more votes from the Moderates than from the left. In 1933 the League contested twenty-three of Glasgow's thirty-seven wards, taking particular care to target Orange-tinged Moderates in working-class wards. Ratcliffe wished to send a clear message to Orange councillors: 'During the two years I have been in the Glasgow Town Council, the Orange members in the Council have been struck dumb on every question pertaining to the Protestantism and Orangeism of Scotland.'[29]

The change in focus was profitable but not for the League. In twelve wards Labour overcame a Moderate vote that was weakened by Protestant candidates. The Moderates had already shown their vulnerability by withdrawing from half-a-dozen safe Labour seats, but that did not help the SPL make an impact. All Ratcliffe's wins were in middle-class Moderate wards. With Labour taking control of the Council it was clear that the SPL impeded Moderate revival.

Yet all was not well with the League, which struggled to find a political identity beyond anti-Catholicism. In 1934 one opponent argued that 'the whole foundation of the SPL programme was to "Kick the Pope", take that away and there is nothing left', an accusation Ratcliffe accepted: "Yes we *do* kick the Pope! That *is* our job! That *is* our programme!"[30] As it became clear that such a limited programme was hindering the Protestant advance, Ratcliffe became ever more dictatorial. By 1934 four of the seven SPL councillors had broken with him, and it was clear that the League was in decline. Under severe pressure, Ratcliffe was persuaded to agree an electoral pact with the Moderates.[31] The League was to be given a clear run against Labour in a number of wards (which seemed to assure Ratcliffe's successful defence of Dennistoun) in return for not standing against Moderates elsewhere. In removing the SPL threat from their suburban heartland, the Moderates got a bargain: Ratcliffe could produce only five candidates and three were in safe Labour wards where they had poor prospects. There was worse to come: a disgruntled Moderate decided to challenge Ratcliffe in Dennistoun. Matthew Armstrong, a long-standing councillor with Orange connections, had lost his seat in 1933 largely through the impact of the League. Armstrong refused to be dissuaded by senior Moderates and stood in Dennistoun as an Independent. The left – excepting an Independent Communist – withdrew and recommended that their supporters back Armstrong. The Orange Order, which had too often been criticised by Ratcliffe to owe him any favours, gleefully endorsed *both* candidates, and Armstrong managed to win allies in the Catholic Union. The press and many pulpits campaigned vigorously for an anti-Ratcliffe vote. The *Daily Record* refused to take the League's adverts. Armstrong won by 300 votes and was accepted back into the Moderate fold with a haste that suggests many had been unhappy with their brief flirtation with Ratcliffe.

Just three years after it had begun, Ratcliffe's political career was at an end. He continued with the Sunday services for a number of years before drifting into fascism and virulent anti-Semitism, just as Britain went to war with Germany and Italy. He died, virtually unknown, in 1947.

It is a small point but it is useful to note how the environment sets the exchange rate of political currency. Sectarian conflict was such a feature of Northern Ireland that being a Protestant party was no obstacle to relevance. In the year where they were seven of them in the council, Ratcliffe's councillors voted against each other more often than they voted together. It turned out they had nothing in common beyond anti-Catholicism (and some did not have much of that). The matters that came before the council could rarely be given a sectarian angle that might have united the SPL councillors and they were not strong enough to influence the agenda. 'Kick the Pope' had enough appeal for a very short period to attract some voters and not to dissuade others attracted by criticisms of council corruption but it was not sufficiently rooted in the social structure to offer coherent answers to the political issues that rose in the routine meetings of the Glasgow City Council.

John Cormack and Protestant Action

With delicious irony, on the very day that Ratcliffe was ousted from the council in Glasgow, Edinburgh, the city that Ratcliffe had decided was barren soil, elected a militant Protestant. John Cormack (1894–1978) had been a League activist in the late 1920s, and had been a leading figure in the Edinburgh Protestant Society, the anti-Ratcliffe organisation that emerged after the League's move westward. Cormack had been raised as an independent Baptist and he became an accomplished outdoor speaker. Edinburgh's militant fringe was a highly fractious scene on the outermost margins of the city's politics and between 1932 and 1934 was divided between Cormack and James Graham, an ex-Catholic recently converted to the No Popery cause. Cormack's faction, formalised from 1933 as the Protestant Action Society (PAS), felt confident enough in 1934 to put forward two candidates in the municipal election, whilst Graham's organisation put forward another. To great surprise Cormack emerged victorious in North Leith, one of the poorest wards in the city, where he defeated a popular Moderate and future Lord Provost. Accused (as Ratcliffe was) of having no genuine policies on the issues affecting local people, Cormack responded bullishly:

We have only one 'plank'. It is a comprehensive one. Wherever in the political life of our country, municipal or national, the Papist beast shows its head we must crush it or, at least, keep it in subjection. Our party is composed of Protestants of every political party who want Protestantism to have its rightful place in our country's jurisdiction, in other words, to defend our Protestant faith.[32]

Defence of that faith demanded the abolition of Catholic state schools; expulsion of Catholic religious orders from Scotland; and the purging of Papists from the armed services and judiciary. In short, Cormack advocated the reimposition of historic Catholic disabilities, utilising the very creedal arguments that the Church of Scotland's campaign studiously avoided. While the Churchmen talked of 'race', the PAS insisted that 'the Reformation must be fought again', viewing their struggle as merely a *local* skirmish between their faith and a global political conspiracy.

In 1935 there were eight Protestant candidates; the PAS ran five, and backed another, with two other organisations standing as well. Taken together, these candidates won 23 per cent of the poll, but there was only one victory, in South Leith, and several close seconds. Success in Edinburgh united militant Protestants around (if not always within) the PAS. In 1936 it pushed Labour into third place and won six more seats. Cormack, like Ratcliffe, struggled to maintain discipline and briefly assumed personal control of the PAS, for which Ratcliffe, without a trace of irony, derided him as a 'Protestant Pope'. In 1937 the PAS contested thirteen wards, and supported former rival James Graham in Dalry. Unusually Cormack stood in both North Leith and Gorgie. It proved a costly error; opponents abused Cormack for his egotism and opportunism. After a tense campaign the only PAS victory came in South Leith, the ward that was to return Cormack the following year. Moderates had strategically withdrawn from some wards, and Protestantism was simply unable to beat Labour in straight fights. In 1938 Cormack won South Leith, but elsewhere the movement polled poorly and, with only one seat, the political career of the PAS was finished. Under the shadow of approaching world war anti-Catholicism shrivelled.

To some degree the PAS shared the same political space as the League in Glasgow: both benefited from discontent over the ruling

Moderates and from the inability of the left to offer a creditable alternative. Both leavened their No Popery with economic populism. But there was a crucial difference. In Glasgow, the League faced a Moderate administration buckling under a Labour advance. In Edinburgh, the Moderate majority was unassailable and the left was sorely underdeveloped. Of the city's twenty-three wards only three could have been described as safe Labour, whilst no fewer than fourteen were solidly Moderate. If the political setting was markedly different, so too was the constituency that was to provide the militant Protestant vote. In Glasgow, the League stood candidates in a variety of wards, from the poverty-stricken East End to the affluent southern suburbs – and it was in the latter that they found the most striking electoral success. Protestant Action, on the other hand, gained almost no support in the middle-class areas of Edinburgh: it was contained within the poorest areas, and in working-class enclaves in more affluent wards. The PAS scored nine of its ten victories in solidly working-class wards – seven of them in Leith. Understanding Leith is central to understanding the PAS phenomenon. Most accounts, however, have focused on events several miles south and west, to a rowdy demonstration in the leafy suburb of Morningside.

Various anti-Catholic demonstrations in 1930s Edinburgh have been described as riots. That widespread violence should occur in Edinburgh (rather than in Glasgow or the Clyde basin) and in one of its premier residential suburbs is seen as symptomatic of the depth of anti-Catholic and anti-Irish sentiment. Yet such an approach overstates the extent of violence and to take it as proof of endemic sectarian sentiments leaves unexplained why there were not violent responses to earlier public displays of Catholicism. It was a planned Eucharistic Congress in 1935 that ignited the sectarian issue. Cormack warned that Edinburgh would learn 'what a real "smash up" was' if the council was to grant an official reception to the Catholic Young Men's Society (CYMS) in the lead-up to the Congress. Protestants were urged to protest, and told in a theatrical aside that 'they could leave the other part of the business to the young fellows'.[33] PAS demonstrations were large and boisterous: around 10,000 gathered for the CYMS protest, and the same for the main anti-Congress demonstration. Many were drawn by curiosity and some by a desire to see some trouble, but it was still a formidable turn-out.

Archbishop Joseph McDonald wrote to Prime Minister Stanley Baldwin to protest that 'priests were savagely assailed, elderly women attacked and kicked, bus-loads of children mercilessly stoned and inoffensive citizens abused and assailed in a manner that is almost unbelievable in any civilised country today'.[34] That depiction has been rather uncritically accepted and repeated by Gallagher and others. Our reading of the contemporary records suggests something far less dramatic. 'Riot' is inappropriate; the protests were characterised more by noisy confusion than by violence. As the Eucharistic Congress approached, the PAS focused its campaign on its closing mass, deliberately drawing its followers away from confrontation on its first two days. However, Cormack found it difficult to control his followers, who staged an impromptu picket of a Catholic rally on the second day, which a nettled Cormack did not attend. Involving 1,500 demonstrators, this incident brought the Protestant movement as close as it came to a riot, although heavy policing ensured that the evening produced scuffles rather than outright confrontation. Nine men were convicted for minor charges and the court imposed deliberately harsh sentences. The following day 10,000 Catholics gathered at St Andrew's Priory in Morningside with perhaps 10,000 Protestants and thrill-seekers gathered outside. Several Catholic buses were stoned – but these were isolated incidents on the fringes of a night characterised by confusion. Cormack desperately tried (and failed) to assert authority over his crowd, which milled around chaotically. Only four people were arrested (and they were harshly sentenced). Small-scale confrontation continued throughout the summer, although the extent of the disorder has been exaggerated in subsequent accounts.

One reason for the exaggeration of PAS violence is the palpable shock experienced in a city unused to sectarian controversy. In Archbishop McDonald's view, the violence was magnified by the absence of an adequately wide and sympathetic recognition of the Catholic experience.[35] These concerns were echoed by Gallagher in his study of Cormack: 'The fact that no major Edinburgh institution such as the Kirk, the police, or the press took a major stand against Cormack or consistently sought to deflect public opinion away from him . . . causes apprehension even at a distance of fifty years.'[36] In fact all three of those institutions were consistent in their hostility to the PAS. In 1935 the *Evening News* and the *Evening Dispatch*

consistently editorialised against Cormack. Sectarian offences attracted harsh punishments, with leniency extended towards Catholics provoked into retaliation.[37] The police handled the militants
with skill, as the absence of any serious and sustained violence
demonstrates. The authorities rightly feared that prosecution would
encourage the militants. In 1936 James Graham was convicted of
breach of the peace, the Sheriff announcing that 'the time had
arrived when the authorities must take up a firm attitude and put
down these disturbances'.[38] Thus encouraged, the authorities preferred charges against Cormack, and, while the prosecution was a
technical success, it gave the PAS an unexpected publicity triumph,
which demonstrated the delicate position in which Edinburgh's
bourgeois institutions found themselves: do nothing and you might
encourage the rabble; act firmly and you give them free advertising.
Mainstream Protestants initially dismissed the militants as un-
churched and unworthy of attention, but in the wake of the
1935 protests Presbyterians were quick to express their disgust
and dismay. A forthright condemnation was written by Revd W.
M. McGregor, the Assembly's Principal Clerk, and published in *Life
and Work* in September 1935. The Kirk's Edinburgh Presbytery
noted that militant success 'had caused much heart-searching and
deep concern to many of their people' and condemned 'all methods
of violence, all interference with personal freedom, and every word
and action which expressed the spirit of hatred' as 'fundamentally
unchristian'.[39] In short, press, civic authorities and mainstream
Presbyterians did oppose the PAS, and the police were extremely
successful in keeping the 'young fellows' in check.

It is easy to understand Gallagher's mistake; Bruce repeated it in
his 1980s work on sectarianism. It is the exaggerated reports that
survive in the most accessible forms and are repeated in the recollec-
tions of the few survivors that Gallagher and Bruce interviewed. The
many condemnations of Cormack's rabble and the more detailed
court reports that give a more accurate picture are neither as eye-
catching nor as accessible. As so often with received wisdom, the
exotic gets repeated and becomes the consensus view. Going back to
the primary sources has shown us that, far from implying anything
that should cause 'apprehension', the actions of Edinburgh's major
institutions show a deep antipathy towards the militants.

Assessing Militant Protestantism

The sudden rise and fall of militant Protestant parties tell us a great deal about the place of anti-Irish and anti-Catholic sentiment in modern Scotland. The rise shows us that antipathy towards Catholics (in particular, 'Irish' Catholics) was widespread in certain circles. The fall shows us that the circles were not wide and the antipathy was not deep. It was not sufficient to sustain militant Protestant politics beyond the highly localised and short-lived phenomena we have described in this chapter. When anti-Catholic and anti-Irish sentiments were used for political purposes, they proved poor ideological tools.

Specific circumstances gave those who wished to peddle a sectarian line the political opportunity to do so. For the anti-Irish faction in the Presbyterian leadership, that opportunity was widespread resentment over Ireland's break with Britain, fears of the power of Labour and the realisation that a united Presbyterianism built with the merger of the Kirk and the UFC would require a united purpose. The disgrace of the Kirk is that it supported, or accepted, or at the very least failed to oppose the campaign. But it failed in its purposes: the united Kirk proved no more successful in asserting social authority than the fractured Kirk, Labour continued to rise in popularity and few amongst the establishment or the wider public were moved by the dire warnings of the Irish menace. Lord Scone very briefly supported Ratcliffe until he stood against a Unionist Party candidate and then withdrew. No other member of the aristocracy or leading industrialist supported Ratcliffe. It is not hard to imagine the sort of support Ratcliffe would have needed (and which his Ulster counterparts received in abundance). Sir John Cargill, the grandson of the founder of Burmah Oil, was a senior figure in the Unionist Association and on the board of Glasgow Rangers FC. He was also a generous supporter of the anti-Labour Economic League. He gave no support to Ratcliffe. Sir Charles Cleland was a leading Unionist and Presbyterian. We may safely suppose he was privately hostile to Roman Catholicism and to Irish nationalist politics. But as Convenor of the Glasgow Education Authority he worked hard to improve Catholic schooling and ensured the smooth transition when Catholic schools were brought in to the system under the terms of the 1918 Education Act. James Brisby, the Ulster-born cleric who supported the 1912 UVF, moderated considerably during his lengthy career on the School Board.[40]

Ratcliffe found that No Popery had electoral appeal only when it could be tied to a localised political crisis: after getting nowhere in Edinburgh he made headway in Glasgow because the Moderate administration was discredited and the Labour opposition was deeply divided. Once Labour had proven itself in office, the political space for the League shrank. In other words, militant Protestantism was an essentially reactive force; its fortunes were hostage to the vagaries of broader processes.

Events in Edinburgh – or more specifically Leith – highlight the inherent marginality of anti-Catholicism in inter-war Scotland. In the Education Authority election of 1925 Leith was treated as a single electoral division. The SPL put forward an ostensibly impressive candidate: Revd John R. Mackay was Professor of New Testament Exegesis at Free Church College, and was to be the Free Kirk's Moderator in 1929–30. Under the proportional voting system used, Mackay received just 481 first-choice votes, coming eighth on a list of ten, with just 7 per cent of the vote. Four redistributions gave Mackay just thirty-six more votes and he was eliminated from the contest. To put this into perspective, a Catholic nominee topped the poll with 1,627 votes, whilst another was elected on transferred preferences. Within a decade, however, Leith was the focal centre of Protestant Action. In the 1934 municipal elections, virtually unknown militant Protestants stood in two of Leith's four wards and together garnered 3,300 votes, eight times as many as Mackay had won across the whole port in 1925. In 1935 the four Leith wards provided 8,000 Protestant votes; in 1936 around 9,500; in 1937 three wards returned 7,500 votes; and even in 1938, when Cormack's decline was irreversible, two Leith wards returned almost 5,000 militant Protestant votes.

It is difficult to explain this without resort to economic factors. There was a tradition of No Popery in Leith. Primmer was a Leither by birth and Ratcliffe a Leither by residence. Like many British ports, Leith had a vibrant independent Protestant subculture. Yet we return to the fact that No Popery did not work in the port in 1925, but was popular a decade later. What had changed was the economic position of Leith. The PAS success hinged on the fact that Edinburgh as a whole escaped the worst ravages of the Depression, and did not qualify for the government's Special Area Assistance schemes. Deprived pockets of the city felt doubly burdened: ignored by Westminster and by the ruling Moderates. Leith had particular grievances after its forced 1920 amalgamation with Edinburgh: many Leithers felt that the administration that had pressed them into surrendering their distinctive identity was now ignoring their economic distress. As a port Leith was acutely sensitive to the global trade crisis, and the idle docks ensured a very high concentration of unemployment. In the mid-1930s Leith contained 25 per cent of Edinburgh's total unemployed, over a third of those who were 'temporarily stopped', and 90 per cent of the unemployed who were 'normally in casual employment'.[41] In ironic counterpoint to its proud and once-affluent history, Leith became an unemployment blackspot with no political influence. The PAS harnessed such resentment. This remarkable turnaround in militant Protestantism's appeal in Leith suggests that anti-Catholicism was less important than more secular, and time-specific, issues. The PAS appealed to workers who felt unappreciated by both Labour and Moderate. As with the SPL, once the worst of the Depression was over, and once the two mainstream parties had begun to address the secular issues that the militants had played upon, the political space for them disappeared.

Conclusion

It is not difficult to find evidence of highly negative attitudes towards Catholics in general (and descendants of Irish Catholics in particular) amongst Scotland's Protestants. But close study of those who sought to make political capital out of these attitudes reveals that anti-Catholicism and anti-Irishness were not popular enough to hold together even a highly localised political movement. A brief contrast with Northern Ireland should make the point. There militant Protestantism and its attacks on Rome represented, and continue to represent, a 'sacred canopy' under which a range of political, religious and socio-economic interests can overcome their differences and work towards shared goals. In Victorian Scotland, on the other hand, militant Protestantism was at best (in the time of Begg) a relatively eccentric hobby horse of some clerics. At worst (as shown by the contesting of Hope's will) it was perceived as an anachronistic and disturbed obsession. By the closing decades of the Victorian era, those few individuals still pursuing a militant Protestant line (such as Primmer) were figures of derision, openly despised by the leading figures in mainstream Protestantism.

One way to see this clearly is to look at the support given by the churches to Ratcliffe and Cormack: almost none. When a movement's own people and the supposed enemy are both defined by religion, the endorsement of the clergy is vital. The very few clergymen who had any enduring association with Ratcliffe or Cormack were marginal figures. We can find only three clergymen who were associated with Cormack. None was linked for long and none belonged to the Church of Scotland. Percival Prescott was a Seventh Day Adventist preacher who was sacked by his Picardy Place congregation. Around 1935 he bought a church that had previously been used by the Congregational Union, the Seceders and the Salvation Army. The congregation for his Evangelical Church numbered fewer than thirty souls.[42] James Trainer served as a locum with the Hermitage UFC in Leith for less than a year. In a public meeting he laid claim to theological expertise and to a career in business; it is likely that he was a retired man and that the 'Reverend' title he used referred only to his licence to work as a locum. We can find no trace of him being ordained or inducted into any major Protestant denominations. The Revd George Goodman was a minister of the UFC who served as a student pastor in Leith in 1933 before moving to Dysart in 1936. The only minister who supported Ratcliffe (and that only briefly) was a Frederick Watson, an elderly Methodist from the north-east of England. He entered the Kirk in 1930 and became minister of Bellshill in 1931.

To balance the record Gallagher lists a number of Presbyterian ministers who spoke out for tolerance and liberalism. He adds: 'These individual efforts deserve not to be overlooked because they show that even in the most perilous years of community relations in lowland Scotland, there were outspoken figures giving a lead in the direction of sanity'.[43] He makes a further point that has been missed in discussions of sectarianism. Because they were not beholden to their members, the Catholic Church's leaders could have done far more than they did to bridge the divide.

In concluding this chapter we come back to the point we made in Chapter 1. It is easy to be struck by evidence of Protestant bigotry (and to exaggerate the violence and popularity of expressions of hostility) and to miss the bigger point that the bigots failed. Hugh Ferguson, John White, Alexander Ratcliffe and John Cormack were not celebrating success; they were protesting against failure. In Scotland, unlike Northern Ireland, there were no very widespread or enduring cleavages that mapped onto, and hence amplified, ethnic or religious divisions. In Ulster, conservative Protestantism operated as a big tent in which Protestants united to defend their economic and political interests. In Scotland, the key issue was class, and here Labour provided a 'secular canopy' within which individuals of all religions and none found their economic interests represented.

Notes

1. T. Gallagher, *Glasgow: The Uneasy Peace* (Manchester: Manchester University Press, 1987), p. 68.
2. Ibid. pp. 42–84
3. T. Gallagher, 'Scotland, Britain and conflict in Ireland', in Y. Alexander and A. O'Day (eds), *Terrorism in Ireland* (London: Croom Helm, 1984), pp. 53–71.
4. Gallagher, *Glasgow*, p. 72.
5. Brisby was an Ulster émigré with an independent ministry based initially in Bridgeton. When his services became too popular for his church, he moved to holding Sunday services in the City Halls in Candleriggs. He had been elected to the Glasgow School Board in 1911 with 84,200 votes but he was beaten by the liberal United Free Church minister and future Labour MP James Barr.
6. J. Buchan, *Mr Standfast* (Harmondsworth: Penguin, 1988), p. 64.
7. Gallagher, *Glasgow*, p. 91.
8. I. S. Wood, 'Hope deferred: Labour in Scotland in the 1920s', in I. Donnachie, C. Harvie and I. S. Wood (eds), *Forward! Labour Politics in Scotland 1888–1988* (Edinburgh: Polygon, 1989), p. 30.
9. It is not germane for our limited purposes but there is an interesting argument between Gallagher and Ian McLean about the effectiveness and power of the Catholic vote; see I. McLean, *The Legend of Red Clydeside* (Edinburgh: John Donald, 1983).
10. F. Blundell, *Hansard*, 191 *HC Deb 5s*: 238; 3 February 1926.
11. S. J. Brown, ' "Outside the Covenant": The Scottish Presbyterian Churches and Irish Immigration 1922–1938', *Innes Review*, 42 (1991), pp. 19–20.
12. J. Burrowes, *Irish: the Remarkable Saga of a Nation and a City* (Edinburgh: Mainstream, 2003), p. 143.
13. Ibid. p. 148.
14. *The Times*, 31 May 1927.
15. G. M. Thomson, *Caledonia or the Future of the Scots* (London: Kegan Paul, Trench and Trubner, 1927), p. 1. His second book gave bizarrely inaccurate figures for Irish immigration.

16. Quoted in Gallagher, *Glasgow*, p. 145.

17. Brown, ' "Outside the Covenant" . . .', pp. 34–5. See *Glasgow Herald*, 20–26 March 1929.

18. *Scotsman*, 24 May 1930.

19. Brown, ' "Outside the Covenant" . . .', pp. 36–7.

20. Quoted in ibid. pp. 39–40.

21. Thomson, *Caledonia* and *The Rediscovery of Scotland* (London: Routledge, 1928).

22. Thomson, *Caledonia*, pp. 56, 16.

23. A. D. Gibb, *Scotland in Europe* (London: Humphrey Toulmin, 1930), p. 55.

24. C. Mackenzie, *Catholicism and Scotland* (London: Routledge, 1936), p. 168. One of the more unusual complaints from Catholics keen to prove Scotland sectarian is that Scotland produced no Catholic novelists. Quite why this should be Scotland's fault is not clear but it also overlooks Mackenzie.

25. For example, Walter Elliott, Tory MP for Kelvingrove and later a powerful Secretary of State for Scotland, backed Catholic demands for an inquiry into the Belfast disturbances of 1935. As Minister for Agriculture, he argued in favour of an accommodation with the newly installed Dublin government of Eamonn de Valera and was influential in preventing a trade war with the Irish Free State; see Gallagher, *Glasgow*, p. 149.

26. A. Muir, *John White* (London: Hodder and Stoughton, 1958).

27. Scottish Reformation Society, *Annual Report 1929–30*.

28. *Edinburgh Evening News*, 29 September 1920; *Glasgow Herald*, 29 September 1920.

29. *Protestant Vanguard*, 6 December 1933.

30. *Protestant Vanguard*, 29 September 1934.

31. W. W. Knox, 'Religion and the Scottish labour movement *c.* 1900–39', *Journal of Contemporary History*, 23 (1988), pp. 609–30. Knox talks of the Moderates signing an electoral pact, which makes the arrangement sound more formal and official than the account given by Gallagher (*Glasgow*, p. 156), who is the source for Knox's comments.

32. *Evening News*, 12 October 1934.

33. *Evening News*, 18 April 1935; *Scotsman*, 27 April 1935.

34. J. Cooney, *Scotland and the Papacy: Pope John Paul II's Visit in Perspective* (Edinburgh: Paul Harris, 1982), p. 20.

35. *The Times*, 6 and 14 August 1935; *Spectator*, 9 and 16 August 1935.

36. T. Gallagher, *Edinburgh Divided: John Cormack and No Popery in Edinburgh in the 1930s* (Edinburgh: Polygon, 1987), p. 187.

37. *Edinburgh Evening News*, 1 August 1935, 6 November 1935.

38. *Edinburgh Evening News*, 30 January 1936, 22 February 1936; *Evening Dispatch*, 10 March 1936.

39. *Edinburgh Evening News*, 2 November 1935.

40. Brisby was elected initially as an independent but re-elected as a Moderate in 1914, 1919, 1922, 1925 and 1928. In 1928 he was elected Vice-Chairman of the Glasgow Education Authority. Two years previously he and his congregation had been accepted into the Church of Scotland.

41. *Edinburgh Evening News*, 7 November 1933, 8 September 1936.
42. Private memorandum in the papers of Archbishop MacDonald, Scottish Catholic Archives.
43. Gallagher, *Glasgow*, p. 143.

3 The Present

Introduction

In this chapter we attempt to assess James MacMillan's claim that Scotland is endemically sectarian. We divide the task into three parts. In the first section we consider a variety of types of discrimination and systematically assess the social-scientific evidence. In the second, we consider the related but separable issue of the extent to which Scots Catholics form a distinctive population. The relationship between distinctiveness and disadvantage is complex. It does not automatically follow that a group that remains separate does so because of the hostility of others; hence we cannot necessarily take isolation as proof of ill-treatment. Nonetheless, we can make something of the reverse. If it is the case that Catholics in Scotland are not that different in political preferences or cultural values, for example, and if they do not claim a clear self-identity as a distinct group, then we can doubt the more extravagant claims that are made about discrimination. In the final part we consider evidence for the extent of anti-Catholic bigotry.

Serious discussion of sectarianism is made difficult by the fact that our tests of the claims must often presuppose exactly what needs testing. In much of what follows we talk about 'Catholics' as if they formed a clearly delineated homogenous group. And in so doing we run the risk of the same racist error that John White made with his 'Irish race'. Social identities are rarely simple. Most of us have a variety of groups to which we can feel attached and we occupy a number of social roles that may vary in salience with time and place. Which of son, father, man, husband, resident of this area, member of this party, attender of that church or citizen of this country constitutes our primary identification is always a matter of context. However, our social analysis has to begin somewhere. We can say nothing if we treat all terms as perpetually problematic.

The difficulty of talking about Catholics and Protestants as if they were distinct types of creatures is obvious as soon as we look at the thing denoted by those labels: religion. Both the Scottish Social Attitudes survey and the Glasgow survey asked people to which religion, if any, they regarded themselves as belonging. Not surprisingly the most commonly chosen religious identity (see Table A3.1 in the appendix) was Church of Scotland (36 per cent in Scotland and 34 per cent in Glasgow). Next came Roman Catholic (14 per cent nationally and 24 per cent in Glasgow). What may be a surprise is that more than a third of the Scottish sample declined to claim any religion; at 37 per cent, the 'no religion' option outstripped the national church. The popularity of 'no religion' is relatively new. Until the late 1960s almost everyone asked claimed a religious label. In a 1974 survey almost a quarter chose 'no religion'.[1] Its present level thus represents a growth of 50 per cent in twenty-five years. In the Glasgow survey, 24 per cent of respondents did not choose a religious identity.

Quite what someone means when he or she claims to be 'Catholic' or 'Church of Scotland' in such surveys is not obvious. It certainly does not imply active involvement. Half of the Church of Scotland identifiers attend church less than once a year and only a third attend once a month or more. For Catholics the figures are 30 per cent for less than once a year and 52 per cent for once a month or more. And these figures, being a summary of what people say about themselves, are likely to be the very top end of the plausible range.

There has been a marked decline in church participation in Scotland as a whole since the 1970s. In 1974, 24 per cent claimed to attend church once a week; in 2001 the figure was 15 per cent. We can see the decline even more clearly if we look at the other end. In 1972 43 per cent said they rarely or never attended church. In

1980 that figure was 50 per cent. By the time of our 2001 survey it had risen to just over 60 per cent. In brief, a clear majority of Scots have no active church commitment.[2]

We can see this decline when we compare church attendance rates for different age groups in the Scottish survey. For example, among the youngest Catholic identifiers 'at least weekly attendance' is only 25 per cent; among those over 55, it is 65 per cent.

Two things follow from this for our subject as a whole. First, when we talk of Protestants and Catholics, few of the people so designated are those things in the strict confessional sense. Second, the period since 1945 has seen a major decline in the popularity (and hence power and influence) of the Christian churches in Scotland.

Disadvantage

LEGAL DISABILITIES

The seventeenth- and eighteenth-century wars over the English (and later the British) throne led to a whole raft of legal penalties being placed on those who did not conform to the national church.[3] Protestant dissenters were punished along with Catholics but were sooner released from restrictions because they were closer in beliefs to the national churches than were Catholics and because they were not seen as an international political threat. The refusal of Quakers to bow to their social superiors might be taken as a challenge to social hierarchies, but there was no chance of them serving as an internal 'fifth column' for an invading French or Spanish army.

The internal stability that followed the crushing of the 1745 rebellion allowed the gradual removal of religious disabilities. The 1793 Relief Act abolished those that banned Catholics from voting, teaching children, buying land or entering the professions, the 1829 Emancipation Act removed almost all the rest, and the final restrictions (concerning the wearing of clerical garments in public) were removed in 1925 and 1926.

There are now only two positions in Scotland that are denied to a Catholic. One is that of Lord High Commissioner (or Queen's representative) to the General Assembly of the Church of Scotland, which the *Catholic Encyclopaedia* dryly describes as 'an office which no Catholic, of course, would desire to hold'.[4] The other is monarch. We might add that this second restriction is not Scottish in origin. It comes from the 1701 Act of Settlement, which was passed by the English Parliament five years before the Act of Union.[5] When former Scottish Secretary Michael Forsyth announced plans to introduce a bill in the House of Lords seeking to amend the act in 1999, members of different political parties and religious denominations joined the campaign for reform. The *Guardian* even launched a legal bid to challenge the Act. Yet, although the late Cardinal Winning urged politicians to confront the constitution's 'grubby little secret', the Catholic Church at UK level did not actively press the government to change the law. In July 2002 the Lord Chancellor announced to peers that the government had no plans to amend or scrap the 1701 Act of Settlement.[6] While accepting that the legislation was 'discriminatory in nature', he pointed out that it was not 'discriminatory in impact' and noted that there were twenty members of the royal family in the line of succession after the Prince of Wales, all of whom were eligible to succeed and were thus unaffected by the existing law. Of course, that might change if William or Harry married a Catholic. But the more obvious point is that all those in line to the throne, and their spouses, are drawn from an extremely small elite of royal and aristocratic families. Hence the 1701 Act of Settlement is irrelevant to the overwhelming majority of Scots, irrespective of their faith.

A few days after Lord Irvine's announcement, the Catholic Church in Scotland called for an investigation into why the Queen has never bestowed her highest Scottish honour of patronage – the Order of the Thistle – on a Catholic.[7] Church spokesman Peter Kearney argued that this neglect was indicative of entrenched anti-Catholic discrimination in the constitution. The Order has only sixteen members, six of whom are hereditary peers. That leaves just ten positions to be filled from people who have been prominent in Scottish public life. When Catholics form less than 20 per cent of the population, this hardly seems like a significant mark of social exclusion. We lack the information to test discrimination claims in all the fields where the Queen may bestow patronage, but from time to time we have come across biographical details that suggest Her Majesty has no policy of excluding Catholics. For example, Lt. Col. Michael Montieth OBE, MC, TD, DL was appointed to the Royal Company of Archers (the Queen's ceremonial bodyguard in Scotland) and was Vice-Lord Lieutenant of Lanarkshire.[8] In 2003

Martin O'Neill, the Northern Ireland-born manager of Celtic Football Club, was awarded an OBE.[9] Catholic businessman Tom Farmer was knighted in 1993. And the retirement of that most prominent of Glasgow Catholic socialist politicians, Paddy Dollan, was marked with a knighthood.

POLITICAL RESTRICTIONS

A common disadvantage placed on unpopular immigrant minorities is denial of the vote. Most Turkish workers in Germany, for example, are excluded from the franchise, as are migrant workers in Switzerland. Catholics have been able to vote since 1793 and to stand for election to the Westminster Parliament since 1829. In practice the majority were excluded, not by religion, but by class. Most men in Britain (and all women) were denied the franchise until the late nineteenth century, by which time a range of archaic criteria had been removed. However, a number of housing, tenancy and residency requirements remained. This, for example, affected the Catholic vote in Glasgow, as so many Irish workers were living in lodgings, were too poor to pay rates or were not registered in any constituency because they moved around so often as casual labour.[10] Such restrictions were removed by 1918, by which time all women over 30 were also given the vote. Ten years later all women over 21 were enfranchised. The minimum voting age for all fell to 18 in 1969.

One small political disability remained until the Labour government introduced the House of Commons (Removal of Clergy Disqualification Act) 2001: the ban on Catholic priests entering Parliament. The change was hurried through to avoid the embarrassing scenario of the Labour candidate for the safe seat of Greenock and Inverclyde being unable to sit in the Commons. Danny Cairns, a former Catholic priest, was duly elected as MP in the 2001 general election.[11] This matter was quickly resolved and few paid note. We should be scrupulous and point out that there is no reason to suppose this restriction was kept in place throughout the twentieth century to offend Catholics. As far as we can find, the matter was never raised before because it is only very recently that any significant number of Catholic priests have given up their religious office and taken up other careers.

The exercise of political power that comes from voting in a

democracy will be considered later. Here we want to consider whether Catholics have been prevented from enjoying careers as political representatives. It has been said, for example, that the main parties have been reluctant to nominate Catholics as candidates for fear of losing Protestant votes. The influence and personal presence of Sir Patrick Dollan in Glasgow in the 1930s suggests that this was not a problem in local politics. But we can certainly find examples where the belief that the electorate might have sectarian preferences has caused party managers to field Protestant candidates, possibly at the expense of Catholic alternatives. The career of Revd James Barr (1861–1949) provides not one, but two, examples. Barr was a UFC minister in Govan who was repeatedly elected to the Glasgow School Board by a largely Protestant electorate but who also enjoyed the confidence of many Catholics and who played a part in the election of Patrick Dollan as councillor for Govan in 1913.[12] Although he was already 61, he was persuaded to stand against and defeat the Orange MP Hugh Ferguson in Motherwell in 1924. It is clear he was selected by Labour Party managers ahead of any Catholic candidate because he was unambiguously socialist, because he had strong support among Catholic party activists and because his religion and office would also attract some Protestants. The fact that he could win both Catholic and Protestant support explains why in 1935 he was again persuaded to come out of retirement, this time to fight the seat of Coatbridge and Airdrie.

We can posit the general principle that, where Labour Party managers are confident of their core support, they will wish to field candidates who have the broadest appeal, and, if they believe voting preferences to follow sectarian lines (with descendants of the Irish who are also Catholic voting Labour and Protestants voting Unionist), Catholics will be disadvantaged in candidate selection for large area elections. Hence we would expect Catholics to achieve parity first in council seats (where the electorate is smaller and good organisation and a well-respected candidate can overcome general preferences) and then in Westminster elections. And this is the pattern we find. Gradually Catholic strength in the manual working class, and hence in the large trade unions, came to be reflected in large numbers of Labour Party local councillors. Gallagher believes that it was only in the 1960s that the proportion of Catholic councillors matched their Labour vote: when about a quarter of councillors were Catholic. Actually parity came a long time before that: out of seventy-six Labour councillors between 1922 and 1931, 21.1 per cent were Catholics: well in proportion to Catholic support for Labour.[13] By the mid-1980s over half of elected Labour members in Glasgow District Council were Catholic.[14] Although we cannot be certain, it is almost certainly the case that, during the lifetime of Strathclyde Regional Council (1975–1995), every leader of the Labour Party and every Lord Provost was a Catholic. A study of Labour councillors in Glasgow in the late 1980s showed that, out of fifty-four surveyed, half described their current religion as Catholic, with several more having been brought up as Catholics.[15]

Iain McLean collected detailed biographical information on all Glasgow Labour councillors from 1909 to the reform of local government in 1974. The percentage of councillors who were Catholic is presented in the appendix (Table A3.2). As we would expect when the number of people involved is small, there are considerable fluctuations, but, overall, while the proportion that is Catholic varies, it is generally around 20 per cent. The data show no evidence that being a Catholic was an obstacle to a successful career in the Labour Party.

What about the picture for Scotland as a whole? Here we are fortunate to have very good information on two very large samples: some 800 local council candidates in 1999 and over 1,000 candidates for the first elections to the Scottish Parliament.

Table 3.1   Religion of council candidates, Scotland, 1999 (%)

Candidates	Candidates' religious background				
	Roman Catholic	Protestant	No religion	Other religion	Total
Conservative candidates	6	77	15	2	100
Conservative vote in 1999	3	89	7	0	99
Labour candidates	19	37	41	4	101
Labour vote in 1999	29	63	7	1	100
Liberal Democrat	6	59	31	4	100
Lib. Dem. vote in 1999	10	80	10	0	100
Scottish National Party	10	39	50	2	101
SNP vote in 1999	14	72	13	2	101

Source: Dr L. Bennie, University of Aberdeen.
Note: In this table, as in subsequent ones, percentage totals may not add to 100, because of rounding.

Before we can judge whether any religious group is under- or over-represented, we need some baseline. As candidates are drawn from the party's membership, the ideal baseline would be the religious breakdown of party membership. This information is not available, so we have calculated the religious breakdown of party preferences as expressed in the 1999 Scottish Social Attitudes survey and presented this figure under the breakdown of candidates. As we can see in Table 3.1, Catholics are under-represented among Labour councillors for Scotland as a whole but Protestants are not the beneficiaries: the category that is over-represented is 'None', which suggests that any explanation is unlikely to involve sectarian discrimination. It is more likely that the difference is a consequence of Catholic voters being concentrated in the urban west coast. The sample reflects party selections for the whole of the country, but Catholics can effectively compete for selection only in those places where they live. Geographical concentration leads to them being slightly under-represented.

Table 3.2   Religion of Scottish Parliament candidates, Scotland, 1999 (%)

Candidates	Candidates' religious background				
	Roman Catholic	Protestant	No Religion	Other Religion	Total
Conservative candidates	13	71	17	0	101
Conservative vote in 1999	3	90	7	0	100
Labour candidates	20	22	57	0	99
Labour vote in 1999	30	61	8	1	100
Liberal Democrat	3	67	27	3	100
Lib Dem vote in 1999	10	77	13	0	100
Scottish National Party	12	33	53	2	100
SNP vote in 1999	17	69	14	0	100

Source: Dr L. Bennie, University of Aberdeen.

The picture for candidates selected to contest the first elections to the Scottish Parliament is given in Table 3.2, and it is much the same as for local council candidates. There is a slight under-representation of Catholics in the Labour lists, but Protestants are below par; it is those with no religion who are over-represented. Surprisingly, Catholics are considerably over-represented in the Conservative Party lists. The party with the greatest relative shortage of Catholics among its candidates is the Liberal Democrats and that is almost certainly explained by the geography of Liberal Democrat strength. Because it is built on its old Liberal base, the party is strongest in the Northern Isles, in the north and north-east and in the Borders – all areas with relatively few Catholics. If Liberal Democrat branches nominated candidates in proportion with the religious composition of their areas, it would produce this sort of pattern.

Finally we come to Westminster candidates. We have no comprehensive data, but our own estimates suggest that in the early 1990s, sixteen out of twenty-two Labour MPs in the industrial heartlands of west and central Scotland were Catholic. That is 73 per cent of MPs Catholic against 24 per cent of Labour voters who are Catholic: a massive over-representation. At Cabinet level, the last two members to fill the post of Secretary of State for Scotland – John Reid and Helen Liddell – were Catholic.

To summarise, there is no evidence that being a Catholic is a disadvantage for a political career in contemporary Scotland.

EDUCATIONAL DISADVANTAGE

In the previous chapters we discussed the origins of Scotland's divided school system. There we noted that the 1918 Education Act had been implemented with very little difficulty and there was a marked improvement in the quality of education for Catholic children. In 1919 there had been a considerable disparity in staff: pupil ratios in Lanarkshire schools. For every one teacher in the non-denominational schools there were 41 pupils; in Catholic schools there were 61. But by 1931 this had converged to 1:34 and 1:40.[16]

The problem of class differences remained, however. Because Catholics were generally poorer than non-Catholics, they were concentrated in the junior secondary schools that did not offer instruction up to the level required for university entrance. Before 1965 only 5 per cent of schools offering senior secondary education were in the denominational sector while Catholics made up 19 per cent of the children of that age group. In 1964 there were only three Catholic schools in Lanarkshire that offered credentials that would allow university access: one in each of Motherwell, Bothwell and Coatbridge. The introduction of comprehensive reform radically changed that: 'within 15 years that number had risen to 13, with new schools or upgraded junior secondaries being able to do the same.'[17] The effects of those changes can be seen very clearly in the history of the Catholic Chaplaincy at Glasgow University. It was opened in 1925. By 1930, when Glasgow was supposedly rent by sectarianism, there were 500 Catholic students out of a student body of 5,531: 9 per cent.[18] By 1956 that number had risen to 700 and in 1972 there were some 2,000 Catholics at the university, which had grown to 9,107: 22 per cent of the student body.

The information on educational attainment in our 2001 survey shows, not surprisingly, that age has an impact on qualifications (older people have considerably lower levels of educational attainment) but that religion does not appear as a major consideration until age is taken into account. Among older Scots, Protestants are better qualified than Catholics at the level of advanced, post-school education (20 per cent compared to 8 per cent). Among middle-aged and younger Scots it is again Protestants who are better qualified but only in so far as they are more likely to hold some sort of qualification. For middle-aged Scots, 81 per cent of Protestants and 72 per cent of Catholics have some sort of qualification; for the youngest cohort, these figures were 94 per cent and 84 per cent. The Glasgow survey shows a similar pattern (especially at a lower overall level of achievement), but the differences between Catholics and Protestants are smaller. Older Protestants are better qualified than Catholics at the advanced level (13 per cent compared to 8 per cent). Among middle-aged Glaswegians it is again Protestants who are more likely to hold some sort of qualification (64 per cent to 60 per cent). But, and this is the crucial point for estimating the extent of change, for the youngest group there is no difference: 83 per cent of both Catholics and Protestants hold some sort of qualification.

These results largely confirm the view that Lindsay Paterson derived from a detailed analysis of the 1997 Scottish election survey. The major change seems to have come with the ending of academic selection for secondary schools in 1965. The impact of comprehensive reform would have been substantial in Glasgow; by 1972 almost all the 25,000 senior Catholic pupils in Glasgow were being educated in comprehensive schools and therefore in an environment that offered greater opportunity to enter higher education.[19] Under the comprehensive system sectarian differences in educational attainment have largely disappeared, although we have provided some evidence at national level to suggest that younger Protestants are still least likely to end up with nothing.

Whatever its other consequences (and we discuss some of these below), the Catholic school system has been a success. Catholics now have access to schools that are as well funded and as educationally effective as those for non-Catholics. In summary, we find no evidence that Catholics are disadvantaged in educational opportunities.

ACCESS TO PUBLIC GOODS

In various ways the modern state is a major source of public goods and services; it is also a major employer. Hence it is therefore worth considering if there is evidence for sectarian discrimination in the operations of local or central government or agencies such as NHS hospitals. We know of no evidence that Catholics are discriminated against in the distribution of social-security payments, unemployment benefits, pensions or the like. Nor that they are denied hospital treatment. And it has not been claimed. The Glasgow survey specifically invited such reports but concluded: 'With regard to unfair treatment by the [Glasgow City] Council and unfair treatment by other public services, perceptions of discrimination do not vary significantly by age, social group, religion or ethnicity.'[20]

We know of no evidence that Catholics have been the victims of discrimination in the allocation of public housing. None appears in the standard sources. We can find only one case of sectarian maladministration and that concerned the reluctance of members of the management committee of the Bridgeton and Dalmarnock Housing Association to rehouse a Catholic family who complained of sectarian abuse.[21] Given the presence of Catholic councillors in the administrations of the councils that have the largest stocks of public housing, it would be a surprise if access to that public good was affected by anti-Catholicism. When Glasgow finally admitted that it could not rehouse its population within it limits and accepted the post-war idea of creating new towns, Sir Patrick Dollan was appointed first chairman of the East Kilbride Development Corporation.

We have had reported to us one claim of sectarian considerations in public housing. Someone who had a temporary job with the West

Lothian Council in the 1960s told us that he was instructed to allocate transfers from Glasgow so that Catholics were posted to Blackburn and Protestants to Livingston. We have no way of testing that claim, but if it was the case the census shows no enduring effects: at 23 per cent, the Catholic population of Blackburn is not unusually high. And at 11 per cent, the Catholic population of Livingston is in the same realm as that for Edinburgh, which provided much of Livingston's growth.

The one recent major claim for sectarianism in public administration concerns the Monklands District Council. In 1992 four Labour members of the council claimed that council leaders were favouring 'Catholic' Coatbridge over 'Protestant' Airdrie by spending almost £500 per head of population in the former while less than £60 per head in the latter, as well as giving council jobs to relatives.[22] After three inquiries into the running of the council and one into the functioning of local Labour Party, no evidence of sectarian discrimination was uncovered, although one inquiry found evidence of nepotism.

Four features of Monklandsgate are worth stressing. First, even if true, the original charge says little about sectarianism, because Coatbridge and Airdrie are not respectively Catholic and Protestant. At best the imbalance is only 60:40. Councillors may have been 'serving their own' but 'their own' here is not especially defined by religion. Second, the putative villains were Catholics, not Protestants. Third, the accusations of pro-Catholic bias were raised by four Catholic councillors.[23] Fourth, and this is the point that must be stressed, detailed investigations did not support the charges. The local journalist who broke the story concerning the investigations into Monklands District Council later complained that the national press had overplayed the sectarian element in order to give the story a more dramatic edge.[24]

As an aside, it is worth noting that even empty charges can be used for political purposes. Two years after the original accusation, allegations of sectarianism were exploited in the build-up to the Monklands East by-election caused by the death of the Labour leader John Smith. A Conservative poster campaign (in pointedly green ink) depicted the Labour Party as a Catholic Mafia, the Scottish National Party (SNP) was accused of playing the 'Orange Card', while Labour canvassers told voters that the SNP would close

Catholic schools and 'create a Northern Ireland'. Although Helen Liddell, a Catholic, was returned as the Labour MP, a 16,000 majority was held by just 1,640 votes from the SNP. It may well be that voters simply did not like an old-style Labour Party official who had worked for the corrupt press baron Robert Maxwell. Or it may be, as Walker suggests, that the SNP was almost the beneficiary of a protest vote by the Protestant electorate, which felt, or, more precisely, was encouraged to feel, that it has been the victim of discrimination. Whatever explains the behaviour of the voters, the campaign showed that the press find sectarianism a useful organising concept for adding drama to an election.

Much state spending takes the form of wages and salaries. We have found some anecdotes of discrimination in hiring in particular council departments, but we can find very little evidence of this being widespread and no claims that it has been since the Second World War. Again the presence of large numbers of Catholic councillors would make it unlikely. One Catholic source told us that Catholics were over-represented in the public sector but added that this was only fitting because of discrimination against them in the private sector.

The growth of the welfare state is important for the status of Scotland's Catholics for two reasons and only one of them directly concerns bigotry. First, whatever the extent of discrimination in the private employment sector, it seems safe to assume it is less in the public sector and this for two reasons: the role of credentials and the role of political power. Access to the more senior jobs requires professional qualifications. A degree of discrimination could still be practised, of course; if there is a surplus of well-qualified candidates, the bigot may systematically chose his co-religionists. Hence there may still be scope for restricting access to well-qualified Catholics, but that scope is restricted by the inability to advance the interests of under-qualified Protestants, which in turn creates more space and hence increases the opportunities for well-qualified Catholics. If credentials are an obstacle to discrimination at the top end of public-service jobs, the political power gained by Catholics through the Labour Party is an obstacle to discrimination at the bottom end.

Second, and this seems the more important point, the expansion of the state liberates certain professions from the financial constraints imposed by the poverty of their clients. So long as teachers were paid by the donations and fees of those they taught, Catholic teachers earned less than non-Catholic ones because the parents who used Catholic schools were typically poorer. Being taken over by the state meant that Catholic teachers could be paid on the national scales. A similar change occurred with the introduction of the National Health Service (NHS). When doctors had to live on the fees of their patients, their incomes were tied to those of the communities they served. The introduction of standardised national pay scales meant that Catholic doctors saw their incomes rise markedly. In brief, the expansion of the state had a levelling effect; by having pay levels and conditions of service set nationally and with little or no regard to the wealth of the people for whom services are provided, income was redistributed. If the council road worker in Skye gets paid the same as his counterpart in Edinburgh, irrespective of the wealth of those who use the roads in question, then those drawn from and serving relatively poorer communities are freed from the inherited disadvantage of their location and clientele.

In summary, we find no evidence of Catholic disadvantage in the consumption of public goods. The only accusation made since the 1970s concerned Catholics unfairly benefiting Catholics and detailed investigation founded that there was no case to answer.

SOCIO-ECONOMIC STATUS

It is worth pursuing the theme of changes in the Scottish labour market post-1945. We have already mentioned the growth of the welfare state. We should also add a major change that is increasingly forgotten as our memories of the Thatcher government that reversed it recede: the nationalisation of essential industries.

At the end of the war, Labour won power on a pledge to take into public ownership the 'commanding heights of the economy'. In 1947 the mines were nationalised. The railways and buses followed in 1948 and in the same year electricity generation became a state enterprise. Steel making was nationalised in 1951, returned to private ownership by the Conservatives in 1955, and renationalised by Labour in 1967. The extent of it varied from industry to industry but nationalisation increased the influence of trade unions and many of the largest unions had an over-representation of Catholics in leadership positions. Some rough idea of the growth of the state sector can be gained from the fact that (though it declined thereafter as a result of the Conservative government's privatisation strategy) in 1979 43 per cent of Scots worked in the public sector.[25]

A related change that should have had a major impact on such labour market disadvantage as was caused by discrimination was the decline of the small locally owned and managed family firm. The history of manufacturing in the twentieth century is a story of increasing centralisation. As it became clear that large sums of capital were required to buy advanced machinery and to service ever-bigger markets, small family enterprises amalgamated into ever bigger companies. As ownership and control shifted from small Scottish towns such as Dumbarton first to Glasgow and Edinburgh and then to London, New York and Japan, so the ability of workers to maintain local preferences was steadily diminished. By 1973 40 per cent of the Scottish manufacturing workforce was employed by English-owned firms.[26] Along with that change in ownership has come greater geographical mobility. It is common for ambitious staff to be sent to the provinces to acquire experience and for people from the provinces to move to the centre to advance their careers, often returning once established. If we add to that the increasing professionalisation of many occupations (such as personnel or 'human-resource' management), with its emphasis on regular training courses and nationally organised workshops and conferences, we would expect that every sort of local preference has become increasingly difficult to sustain. A small example of the consequences of this increasing entanglement of Scottish business in national and international enterprises is given by the journalist Harry Conroy. He mentions that the Glasgow office of the national paper for which he worked for a long time in the 1960s had no Catholic photographers. 'The first Catholic to appear on the photographers' desk came in at the top as associate picture editor. The English management of the newspaper who were not party to such [sectarian] prejudices appointed him. Needless to say things changed after that.'[27]

This background leads us to expect that the effect of discrimination in the labour market should have declined. The improvements in Catholic education should have removed the main self-generated disadvantages. Hence differences in employment prospects and

careers of Catholic and non-Catholics should have declined. This is
the conclusion of Paterson's analysis of information collected in the
Scottish School Leavers' survey. In 1980 a third of those leaving non-
denominational schools had fathers in white-collar work, but the
corresponding figure for those leaving Catholic schools was only 16
per cent. But by 1994 the difference had halved: for state schools the
white-collar father percentage had risen to 37 per cent but for
Catholic schools it had risen to 29 per cent.[28]

What does the evidence of our Scotland and Glasgow surveys
show? In Scotland as a whole, Catholics are more likely than
Protestants to work in lower-status semi-routine or routine jobs:
for managerial and professional positions, the relationship is
precisely reversed. However, it is important to divide the survey
sample into age cohorts.[29] And, as Table 3.3 shows, the greatest
differences in work status are found with older Catholics
(particularly men). Among those aged 55 and over, only 26 per
cent of respondents raised as Catholics but 49 per cent of those
raised in the Church of Scotland were in non-manual occupations
(a difference of 20 points).[30] Among younger respondents the
difference was small (5 percentage points) and statistically insignificant, confirming the impression derived from those for educational
qualifications. What was once a major sectarian divide has been
reduced markedly.

Table 3.3   Religion of upbringing by class and age, Scotland, 2001 (%)

Age group	Percentage of each group in a non-manual occupation				
	Roman Catholic	Church of Scotland	No religion	Other religion	All
18–34 years	58	63	45	65	58
35–54 years	47	58	45	62	55
55+ years	26	49	33	63	48

Note: Non-manual refers to 'Employers & Managers', 'Intermediate Occupations', 'Small
Employers and Own Account Workers' in the National Statistics Socio-economic
Classification 2000.
Source: Scottish Social Attitudes survey (N = 1,597).

But is it sensible to make comparisons between Catholic and
other older respondents living throughout Scotland? Fewer than

one in twenty Scots in the north of the country comes from a Catholic family. And most Catholics, particularly older Catholics, live in the ageing industrial heartlands of west central Scotland, in areas that are often characterised by poor socio-economic profiles.[31] The Glasgow survey (see Table A3.3) allows us to shed light on the relative socio-economic fortunes of Catholics and Protestants in the part of the country where Catholics are most likely to live. We find differences in occupational status that are related to religious upbringing, but, in a very similar fashion to the national data, they are closely associated with age. The differences reach statistical significance (that is, are likely to reflect real differences and not just quirks of sample selection and statistical techniques) only for the oldest age group, where 30 per cent of Kirk identifiers and only 14 per cent of Catholics have non-manual profiles. Such differences in socio-economic status diminish through the middle age group (where it is only 7 points) and are again small for the youngest age group: at 5 percentage points.

These results come from sample surveys and it is always possible that they are unrepresentative of the population as a whole (though unlikely given that they were conducted by experienced professionals). The great virtue of the 2001 national census is that it contains information about social class for the entire population (see Table A3.4). The data that have so far been released are a little awkward to interpret for two reasons. There is some distortion for the youngest age group because the census treats social class as a household measure and attributes the class of the 'household reference person' (the person who completed the form – usually the main wage-earner) to all members of the household. If, as our surveys suggest, there is upward mobility over the generations, this will be under-reported in the census. There is also some difficulty interpreting social class E, which, in addition to households where the reference person is in the lowest grades of employment, includes those where the reference person is long-term unemployed, living on state benefits or over the age of 74 and living in rented housing. So we should be cautious about inferring much from the data for the oldest age cohort. But these reservations are offset by the value of the number of cases: for the cohort of those aged 35–54 the census tells us about 1.5 million people.

Table 3.4   Religion of upbringing by class in middle age cohort,
                 Scotland and Glasgow City, 2001 (%)

	Roman Catholic	Church of Scotland	No religion	Other religion	All
Scotland					
AB	22	24	19	30	24
C1	27	29	26	29	28
C2	17	20	20	16	18
D	21	19	24	16	19
E	13	9	12	9	10
	100	101	101	100	99
Glasgow City					
AB	16	17	18	23	18
C1	23	25	25	27	25
C2	15	15	13	13	14
D	23	21	20	17	21
E	24	22	24	21	22
	100	100	100	101	100

Note: The results are for 35–54-year-olds. Category AB includes managerial and
professional occupations. E includes lowest grade workers and those who are on state
benefits or unemployed. Table A3.4 provides more details.
Source: GRO Scotland, Census, 2001.

As can be seen from Table 3.4, the picture of few socio-economic
differences between middle-aged Catholics and Protestants is confirmed by the 2001 census for Scotland as a whole and, more
importantly, for Glasgow in particular. Differences in the proportions of Catholics and Protestants in white-collar occupations are of
the order of 5 percentage points or less for the middle age cohort.

Taken together, the Scottish Social Attitudes survey, the Glasgow
City survey, and the national census paint a clear picture: religious
differences in social class are largely restricted to older Scots.

It is important to know if such figures should be read as religion
influencing social class or as social class influencing religion. Because
our data are only a one-off snapshot, we cannot follow the fate of a
single group over time and thus see clearly what causes what (although
we have attempted to control for the direction of causation by using
religion of upbringing). There is also an element of questionable
extrapolation in our use of the three age groups to talk about change
over time. Hence the results from both surveys could mean that the

patterning of socio-economic differences between Catholics and Protestants are a residue of sectarianism and represent processes that no longer operate, or they could mean that there are currently sectarian forces at work that produce their effects only late in the life course. This seems unlikely. All the anecdotes about discrimination cite the identity of the school attended or some other childhood characteristic (such as membership of the Boys Brigade) as the bigot's clue to religious identity. The handicap is apparent and effective at the start of the working life. It is hard to see how young Catholics who acquire a high-status profession at age 25 should then become downwardly mobile in later life to an extent that would show up in our rather crude data.

One drawback to our concentration on the relative fate of Protestants and Catholics is that it may blind us to other significant effects of religious upbringing. In many of our detailed analyses of the links between religious upbringing and education and social class, it is often the group of those who said they were raised with 'no religion' that does most badly. As can be seen in Table 3.3, for the youngest age cohort, those raised with no religion are least likely to have middle-class jobs (and are further behind Catholics than Catholics are behind those raised as Church of Scotland). Why this should be the case is not obvious, but the finding is important because, whatever it is that explains why people raised with no religion should be socially disadvantaged, it is very unlikely to be discrimination. Even if we believed that people with power and influence would want to discriminate against those not socialised in any religion, it is hard to conceive of a mechanism that would allow such persecution. Hence we must conclude that the socio-economic fate of a significant number of Scots is being influenced by religious background (or, to be more precise, lack of it) in a way that does not involve discrimination. If that is so for one group, it may also be so for all groups. In brief, broadening the analysis from Catholic–Protestant comparisons to detailed comparison of all the religion categories offers some good reason to be cautious about interpreting any of the patterns we find as strong evidence for discrimination.

Perceptions of Discrimination

As well as trying to compare fortunes in the labour market, we have tried to gauge people's perceptions. The Scottish survey asked if respondents believed that 'being a Catholic limits employment or promotion opportunities in present-day Scotland'. Catholics are more likely than non-Catholics to think that there remains a disadvantage: one half of those raised as Catholics feel their religion still matters; and a third of other respondents also feel that being Catholic matters. When we asked if respondents had themselves experienced discrimination because of their religious identities, the total fell to 18 per cent of Catholics, but that is compared to only 3 per cent of other respondents.

This reminds us of the power of shared perceptions. Two-thirds of those who thought discrimination was a problem did not feel that they had suffered it themselves. And when we break those responses down by gender and age, we find it is Catholic men who think they have been discriminated against, and particularly older Catholic men.

The Glasgow survey asked people if they thought it common for someone to be turned down for a job or promotion for religious reasons. The majority of both Catholics and Protestants believe that such discrimination exists and that it is very common (around 15 per cent) or quite common (around 38 per cent). That this is not the effect of discrimination is plain from the fact that the belief is equally likely to be held by Protestants as by Catholics. Catholic and Protestant views remain similar when broken down by age, gender, social class and education level.[32]

But again, when we move from general expectations to personal experience, we find the same change and in the Glasgow study it is even more abrupt than for Scotland as a whole. When asked about their direct experience of discrimination in the labour market, only 1 per cent of the entire sample (11 people out of 1,029) said they felt they had been turned down for a job in the last five years because of their religion; exactly the same proportion reported being unfairly treated at work for the same reason. Not all of these people were Catholics. Only four of those who thought they had been denied jobs and only three of those who thought they had been treated unfairly were Catholics. Two people said both, so the total of Catholics who claimed to have experienced discrimination was five and an equally large number of those who felt they had been victimised were people with no religion.[33]

At the risk of labouring the point, we will spell out the gulf between perception and experience. Although seventy-eight Catholics thought that religious discrimination in the workplace was quite or very common, only five claimed to have experienced any. That is, 98.3 per cent of Catholics in the Glasgow survey declined the chance to claim to have been victims of discrimination.

Where a significant difference between Catholics and Protestants was found was in what we might think of as career aspirations. Respondents were asked if they had 'ever felt religion was relevant to what jobs you could apply for'. Although the total numbers agreeing were very small, Catholics were more than twice as likely as Protestants to believe that there were jobs that they could not apply for: 14 per cent to 6 per cent. And this sense of a religious divide within the job market persists when we compare Catholics and Protestants of specific social class, age, gender and education level. For example, both Catholic men and women are more likely to feel that way when compared to their Protestant counterparts, and very similar differences are found between Catholics and Protestants within age and social-class groupings. Indeed, when gender and social-class differences are controlled for age, both younger and older Catholic men are still more likely to feel that some jobs cannot be applied for. Similarly, older working-class Catholics are also more likely to feel that way. Within different social groups, perhaps the most striking religious difference is to be found among younger well-educated Glaswegians under the age of 45 years; 21 per cent of such Catholics but only 8 per cent of such Protestants thought religion was relevant to what jobs could be applied for. Unfortunately the survey did not press the question to find out just what jobs people had in mind.

It is not immediately obvious why expectation of discrimination should so far outstrip the reality. Part of the explanation, as far as Catholics go, is probably the transmission of family experiences. People are told stories by their parents and grandparents; what one generation believes to be the case may be strongly shaped by what was the case for their parents. If this is the explanation, then we would expect that perceptions will gradually change also – about thirty years behind the reality.

If people expect something to be the case then it can easily influence their perceptions. Patricia Walls and Rory Williams interviewed seventy-two adult west coast Scots of Irish descent about their experience of workplace discrimination. Although the authors present the data as evidence of widespread sectarianism, almost all the quotations (and we must assume the authors have used the quotes that best make their case) report only a religious imbalance in the workforce, usually at some time in the distant past, and say that *someone else* told them that discrimination used to be common. It is a pity the interviewers did not press their respondents on how they knew the religious composition of large work units. It is also a pity that they did not ask each speaker who said that discrimination was common why, if that was the case, they had not personally experienced any.[34]

One reason why perceptions may be lagging behind reality is that the regular reporting of claims of discrimination and the high profile given by the media to assertions such as those made by James MacMillan sustain a myth. There is an obvious parallel in old people's fear of crime. All the evidence shows that old people are far less likely than others to be the victims of crime. Nonetheless they selectively attend to the reports of attacks on old people and suppose them to be commonplace. Certainly an accurate appreciation of reality is not helped by public pronouncements such as that of Unison, Scotland's largest public-sector trade union. In its response to the public consultations on Donald Gorrie's bill to make religious hatred a criminal offence, it cited one part of the Glasgow survey data – 'that a quarter of respondents felt that sectarianism was common in employment decisions' – but did not mention at all that almost none of the respondents claimed to have experienced this supposedly widespread social phenomenon.[35]

The gulf between perception and reality may be better understood if we distinguish between bigotry and effective discrimination: they may decline at different rates. Let us construct an illustration. In 1920 the personnel manager of a Vale of Leven factory is a militant Protestant who both expresses anti-Catholic sentiment and denies Catholics jobs. He expresses bigotry and effectively discriminates. In 1960 the son of the first bigot, who has inherited his father's sentiments, still works in the same factory but he has not inherited his father's power. Hiring is done by a professional implementing policies formulated in the USA. Catholics are no longer denied jobs but they still hear bigoted opinions. Although Catholics are no longer denied opportunities (that is, the reality that is later reflected in surveys of socio-economic status has changed), they underestimate the extent to which the world has changed because they still perceive bigotry. Any one person may know that his or her career has not been blighted but may suppose this is unusual and that unknown co-religionists have suffered discrimination.

It takes us back a stage but, just as we decoupled discrimination and bigotry in trying to explain why the beliefs of Glasgow survey respondents about the labour market are so far from their own experiences, so we can usefully separate discrimination and long-term disadvantage. Although it is hard to imagine how there could be widespread anti-Catholic discrimination without Catholics remaining of lower socio-economic status than non-Catholics, it is possible to imagine a model of limited discrimination having no long-term effect on career prospects. Suppose that the demand for labour exceeds supply. Someone may be denied a post in one firm because of his or her religion but readily find a similar job elsewhere. Discrimination would be felt but it would not damage socio-economic status.

One possible version of that story is that, while particular occupations (and hence social statuses) are not closed to Catholics, certain sectors of the labour market are or have been. For example, a Catholic accountant might be barred from banks and insurance houses but find a job in an oil firm or a local authority. It is certainly noticeable that many of the stories of discrimination concern banks and finance houses. Gallagher tells the story of the Coatbridge Catholic head teacher who claimed to discover that all the local banks operated a ban on recruiting Catholics.[36] Other sources have asserted that senior management in Scottish finance is almost exclusively Protestant. We have no evidence for this claim and, even if true, it may well reflect not sectarianism but social-class exclusion. The top levels of 'old' capitalism recruit from a small and relatively closed world of families with close kinship ties and a common educational background in private schools. Until recently, Catholics would have found it hard to enter this world, not because they were Catholic but because they were not old elite.

Another sector sometimes mentioned is the law. The celebrated Glasgow solicitor Joe Beltrami said:

> In 1950 I was trying to get an apprenticeship as a lawyer and I tried 24 firms and was rejected each time. At the time, I didn't realise

the reason but each firm asked me which school I went to and would then tell me that they would write to me. It is not so bad now but there is still this great divide between Catholics and Protestants in the legal profession.[37]

Interestingly Gallagher offers a different explanation and assessment. Although he is speaking specifically about entry to the profession of barrister rather than solicitor, Gallagher explains the paucity of Catholics by the poverty of their families. He notes that entry to the legal profession required considerable financial investment in the form both of direct costs and of deferring gratification for a long period. He further says:

> For all its elitist characteristics the Scottish legal profession passed the religious test regarding those Catholics seeking to breach its citadels with flying colours. It did not close ranks to keep Catholics out but accepted those with the necessary qualifications and persistence into its elitist ranks.[38]

Gallagher also undermines the general view that the professions were difficult to penetrate by approvingly quoting James Gordon, the entrepreneur and founder of Radio Clyde, who said: 'in my younger days the idea of going out and starting your own business in the 1950s would have taken many people aback . . . the professions were regarded as the natural post-university outlet for Catholics.'[39]

Our data are not sufficiently detailed to test the claims about the proportion of Catholics in specific sectors but we can test a related claim made by James Conroy, who wrote: 'a closer look at notions of social mobility is likely to reveal that Catholics have been successful at certain (largely caring) professions but this in itself is no guarantee of the absence of establishment discrimination.'[40] We are not sure what would count as a 'guarantee of the absence' of something but we can compare the proportions of Catholics and others in working in the public and private sectors and it shows no statistically significant difference.[41] We would certainly expect some differences in career patterns even if no discrimination was involved because, as we have already noted, until recently Catholic schools were much less likely than their state-sector equivalents to promote technical education. However, we suspect the explanation for Conroy's guess is simply that he is supposing the experience of his friends to be unusual. As the caring professions have expanded relative to man-ufacturing, they will have become more common careers for all Scots. A more definitive answer must await detailed analysis of the 2001 census, but in the meantime we can say with some certainty that, in the Scottish 2001 survey, Catholics are not under-repre-sented in the private sector.

Finally in this discussion of the reality and perception of discrimina-tion at work, we would like to suggest a novel explanation of why so many people get it wrong. Above we questioned the wisdom of treating lay people as experts in the religious composition of their workplaces: how do they know? But there is an even bigger problem lying behind that one. Before we can think that a certain sort of person is under-represented, we must possess a notion of what the proper extent of representation should be. For example, the proposition that women are under-represented in the higher ranks of the police rests on establishing not just (a) what proportion of officers of superintendent and above are female but also (b) what proportion should be women. That baseline could be the proportion of all officers that are women or the proportion of all adults of working age who are women.

For someone to believe that Catholics are under-represented in this or that profession, workplace or grade, he or she must have a prior notion of what degree of representation would be expected if religion was not at all a consideration. We see no good reason to suppose that lay people get this right and some very good reasons why they would get it wrong.

According to the 2001 census, Catholics form 16 per cent of the population. Catholics are concentrated in the Lowlands of Scotland, but even in Glasgow city they form only 29 per cent of the population. Were they properly informed, people would think there was a shortage of Catholics in any workplace only if, for every ten people with whom they worked, only one or two were Catholic. Three would be par and more than three would be over-representation. We suspect that many Lowland Scots have a very different imagined baseline. For the following reasons they are very likely to overestimate the Catholic population.

First, although the Catholic school sector is much smaller than the state system, the relative size of the two is not usually a topic in its own right and most media reports present church and state sectors as equal alternatives.

Second, as we will see shortly, because decline set in earlier for the Church of Scotland than for the Catholic Church, Catholics form a large part of the church-going population. About 35 per cent of Scots who attend church are Catholic, as compared to 40 per cent who are Church of Scotland. The remaining 25 per cent are divided amongst a large number of small organisations and hence are very easy to overlook. If one's image of relative size is shaped by impressions derived from church-related activity (or such second-hand reports as TV dramas and documentaries), one is quite likely to think of the Catholic Church as the equal of the national Church.

Third, that impression of equal size will be reinforced by any contact with social institutions such as hospital, prison and university chaplaincies. As we describe below, it is common for organisations that have to employ clergy to start with one Church of Scotland and one Roman Catholic representative.

Fourth, and we also discuss this in more detail shortly, because it takes a number of distinctive positions on matters of public interest (such as abortion and contraception) and because it has a structure that allows it to present those positions forcefully, the Catholic Church has a disproportionately great impact on the media.

Finally, we might add the impact of football. As the Glasgow city survey showed, when many people think of sectarianism, they have in mind the rivalry between Rangers and Celtic: clubs of equal size and success who are always treated as two parts of a matching set.

If it is the case that people implicitly think of Catholic and Protestant as equal alternatives, they will overestimate the Catholic population of their areas. They will thus frequently and mistakenly believe that Catholics are under-represented and will be liable to accept the most dramatic and easy-to-grasp explanation of that perceived disparity: discrimination. That might well explain why so many Scots think sectarian discrimination is commonplace while so few of them claim to have themselves suffered it.

In summary, Catholics who entered the labour market between 1940 and 1965 suffered considerable disadvantage relative to non-Catholics. Catholics who entered the workforce in the 1980s did not. We have to be cautious in guessing an explanation for that initial disadvantage, and the subsequent change. All too easily difference is taken to be the result of discrimination and other possible explanations overlooked. The quality of education is likely to be a major consideration. The state funding of Catholic schools post-1918 did something to make up the ground church schools had lost by declining to join the 1872 structure of national schooling, but the social class of parents continued to be a disadvantage (and advantage) inherited by all children from their parents, and, as the immigrant Irish entered the labour market at the bottom, that handicap would have been overcome only slowly. As Lindsay Paterson has argued, the introduction of comprehensive secondary schooling did much to remove inherited disadvantage from all Scots (and thus particularly from Catholics).

We should also stress that not all discrimination is sectarian in intent. What the Monklandsgate investigation found was not sectarianism but *nepotism*: unfairly advantaging family. In the 1960s there was a spate of scandals involving Glasgow councillors and contracts and drinks licenses.[42] Although the net effect was sectarian in the sense that bent councillors were advancing the interests of Catholics, religion was only coincidentally implicated. The intended recipients of corrupt assistance were family and friends. What the major changes in the Scottish economy did was to reduce the opportunities for unfairly helping 'yer ain folk'.

Public Protection

As late as the 1960s, blacks in the southern states of the USA were patently denied the protection of the law. They were routinely subjected to actual as well as verbal harassment and the police and the courts did little to protect them. Only when large numbers of young white students from the northern states became involved in civil protests in the early 1960s did the scandal of racist police and courts come to the attention of the USA at large and provoke a federal response. In Chapter 1 we cited some examples of similar failings in nineteenth-century Scotland and in Chapter 2 we discussed the accusation that the Edinburgh authorities were slow to clamp down on the disturbances created by John Cormack's Protestant Action.[43]

Is it still the case that Catholics are denied the protection of the state? The specific issue of Old Firm football violence will be examined in detail in the next chapter. It should be stressed that even those who claim that Catholics are disproportionately victimised do not assert that the Scottish police and justice systems work any less hard to make villains 'amenable' for those offences. That is, the claim is not the major one that could be made for the Royal Ulster Constabulary in Belfast in 1970, the Mississippi police in 1964 or the Greenock police in 1852: that agents of the state deliberately victimised Catholics. Nor is it asserted that the Scottish state is 'institutionally sectarian' (to paraphrase the criticism made of the Metropolitan police in the late 1990s) in not properly pursuing the perpetrators of sectarian violence. It is the minor one that Catholics are victimised because of their religion and hence that, because they have that characteristic and the majority do not, Catholics are more often victimised than others.

The Glasgow survey asked people if they had been the victims of crimes of various sorts over the previous five years. It found:

> no significant difference with regard to the level of crime experienced by respondents who classify themselves as Catholics and those who classify themselves as belonging to a Protestant faith. However, people who classify themselves as having no religion . . . were more likely than both Protestants and Catholics to report having been physically attacked, threatened or to have been the victim of another form of harassment in the last five years.[44]

The explanation is age. Religion was not a consideration but generally the young were more likely to be victims than the elderly and the 'no-religion' people were disproportionately young. Those who had been victims were offered a variety of possible reasons for being victimised. As Table A3.5 shows, only 5 per cent of those who had been attacked, 2 per cent of those whose property had been vandalised and 5 per cent of those who had been threatened thought that religion was the reason. Gender, sexual orientation and country of origin were cited as often as religion as the reason for physical attacks and all those came a long way behind 'area where you live'. In total, less than 1 per cent of respondents thought they had been attacked because of their religion and one of the seven individuals was non-Christian. We should stress that these are data from the survey of Glasgow: the place where sectarianism is most likely to be found.

In brief, there is no evidence that Catholics are denied the protection of the state or that religious identity is a significant source of victimisation.

THE PUBLIC STANDING OF THE CATHOLIC CHURCH

One way in which Catholics in Scotland could be discriminated against would be for their culture to be denied social prestige. In the nineteenth and early twentieth centuries, the varieties of Presbyterian Church were taken by social elites and the common people as being the proper form for Scottish religion and the Catholic Church was treated as an alien presence. The state funding of Catholic schools suggests that Catholicism is now accepted as an entirely legitimate religion, but it is worth considering how the Church is treated more generally.

One useful mark is presence in chaplaincies. Prison and hospital chaplains are appointed and paid by state agencies and offer a symbolically potent opportunity for the state to deny legitimacy to Catholicism. Out of 519 chaplains employed by the NHS in 2003, 31 per cent were Catholic. Just over a third of prison chaplains were Catholic.[45] When only 16 per cent of the population is Catholic, this is a considerable over-representation. There is a simple explanation. If a prison or hospital is to have more than one chaplain, the second one will be a Catholic priest. As most units have only two or three, over-representation is inevitable.

One field in which the Catholic Church did take a long time to achieve parity was religious broadcasting. From its foundation the BBC was keen to broadcast religious talks and services. Until the 1950s church services that were broadcast were usually those of the national church (thus Church of Scotland north of the border and Church of England south of it). The Catholic Church had a number of reservations about broadcasting. As it regarded its services as sacraments, it was reluctant to have them treated as spectacles that people heard or watched rather than participated in. The problem was a version of Dean Ryle's famous refusal to have the wedding of the Duke of York and Lady Elizabeth Bowes-Lyon broadcast because men in public houses might listen with their hats on![46] And the BBC was not keen on services in Latin. The Church also had a problem with the BBC's idea of religion. The founder of the BBC, John Reith, was not a committed Christian and saw religion largely in terms of its social function: encouraging an uplifting patriotism. Committed Christians from all parts of the theological spectrum were critical of lowest-common-denominator 'BBC religion'.

Eventually the Catholic Church and the BBC found ways of living with each other and, in 1953, Fr Angelus Andrews was appointed to the BBC's Religion Department staff. Since then the Church has been a full participant in Britain's religious broadcasting. In 2003 the vice-chairman of the Central Religious Advisory Committee, which advises both the BBC and the ITV companies, was the Roman Catholic Bishop of East Anglia, the Rt Revd Peter Smith. A number of Catholic priests have become popular broadcasters in Scotland. Fr Andrew Monaghan presents Radio Forth's Open Line phone-in. For many years in the late 1990s Fr John Fitzsimmons occupied a BBC Radio Scotland Sunday morning slot. In brief, the Catholic Church has enjoyed parity of access to the British airwaves since the 1960s.

A further sign of parity of esteem is the full incorporation of St Andrews, the Catholic teacher training college, into the University of Glasgow in the 1990s. Among his evidences for the endemic sectarianism of contemporary Scotland, James MacMillan cited the fact that one member of the university's education faculty had publicly objected to this merger. He overlooked the larger point that the merger had gone ahead and had been welcomed by the rest of the university and by Scotland's higher education community. The ties with the Church were further cemented when, notwithstanding the Church's unpopular attitudes to abortion, the university accepted £250,000 to create the St Kentigern chair in child welfare.

We might also note that the Church has been successful in promoting its interests in discussions over government policy. Lynch describes in some detail the way that church officials were able to influence plans for local government reorganisation in the mid-1990s so that changes in local-authority structure did not disrupt school catchment areas.[47]

For those who maintain that most Scots are bigots, all this could be dismissed as grudging compliance with universalistic criteria by people who would really like to punish the Popish heresy but are prevented from doing so by the state. However, there is ample evidence of Scottish elites going out of their way to show approval of the Catholic Church. Despite the Catholic Church's refusal to accept the Church of Scotland as an equal, the Kirk has since 1971 invited the Catholic Church to send an official observer to its annual General Assembly. In 1975 it invited Archbishop (later Cardinal) Winning to address the assembly. When the Pope visited Scotland in May 1982 he was greeted by the Moderator of the General Assembly of the

Church of Scotland and other Protestant church leaders in the forecourt of New College in Edinburgh. Few locations could be more significant. New College is the main theology hall of the Church of Scotland. It was formerly the ministerial training college of the Free Church (and hence a place where the Victorian anti-Catholic James Begg would often have been heard). It houses the Church's General Assembly. And the meeting took place under the eyes of the statue of John Knox, the leader of Scotland's Reformation. It is worth adding that militant Protestant demonstrations against the papal visit were trivial: barely 100 people demonstrated at the Mound and they were drawn from all over the UK.

Since the creation of the Scottish Parliament, there has been no shortage of public official approval of the Catholic Church. On 4 December 2000, Henry McLeish, Scotland's First Minister, and John Reid, the Westminster Parliament's Secretary of State for Scotland, met the Pope to commemorate the 400th anniversary of the pontifical Scots College in Rome. In February 2002, when Mario Conti was enthroned as Archbishop of Glasgow, the service was attended by Jack McConnell, the First Minister, and Helen Liddell, the last Secretary of State for Scotland.

When the operating procedures for the Scottish Parliament were being determined in 1999, there was considerable debate about whether the day's business should be opened with some sort of prayers. It is a mark of how much had changed since the 1950s that there was never any suggestion that Presbyterianism should be given a privileged position.

It is hard to argue that the Catholic Church has been denied access to the mass media. As Harry Reid, a former editor of the Glasgow *Herald* and the author of a dispassionate study of the Kirk, argues, because the Catholic Church is hierarchical and has its senior officials in place for long periods, it is able to present a very clear message when the views of the Church of Scotland (which rotates its leadership and has a much more democratic and egalitarian structure) are opaque.[49] Especially during the regime of Cardinal Winning, journalists were always able to get 'the Catholic line' but had considerable difficulty finding someone who could speak authoritatively for the Presbyterian churches.

It is certainly the case that the Catholic Church is treated with far greater respect than are the conservative strands of Presbyterianism.

The Free Church and Free Presbyterian Church are routinely treated as a threat or as an anachronism; either their Calvinism is a danger to liberal values or their people are a joke. The only case we can find in recent years of any church being denied planning permission for a new church building concerns not the Catholic Church but the Free Presbyterian Church of Ulster. In the early 1990s, a small group of disaffected evangelical members of the Church of Scotland in Gardenstown, Aberdeenshire, invited Ian Paisley's Free Presbyterian Church to supply them with a minister. The work was so successful that they applied for planning permission to erect a church building and it was denied. It was clear from the objections to the planning permission bid and from comments of councillors that locals objected to Paisley, to an Ulster connection and to evangelical Protestantism. Only after two years of argument was the request granted.

In his scatter-gun essay, James MacMillan claims as evidence of Scottish hostility to the Catholic Church what he takes to be overenthusiastic reporting of the sex-abuse scandals that came to the fore in the late 1990s. It is, of course, hard to know what would count as an appropriate level of reporting, but we see no evidence that the Scottish media have been harder on Catholic priests who abuse children in their trust than on perverts of other religions or none. We also note that the sex and abuse scandals that have rocked the Church have been brought to light, not by malicious Protestants, but by their Catholic victims. And, as one might expect, those who have been most active in criticising the Church are ex-Catholics. For example, *The Magdalene Sisters*, a powerful film dramatisation of the abuse of children in the Church's care, was directed not by a Protestant but by the Scots Catholic actor Peter Mullen.

MacMillan also complains that the pre-Reformation part of Scotland's history is deliberately hidden: that Scottish culture is taken to start in 1560. He is right about our neglect of the past but he is wrong to take it personally. In this, if nothing else, Scots are even-handed: ignorance of Scots history is universal and ecumenical.

Distinctiveness
LIVING TOGETHER
If Scotland really is endemically sectarian, we would expect this to show up in residential segregation; Protestants would want to

exclude Catholics and Catholics would avoid living next to those who did not want them. In Northern Ireland, Protestants and Catholics live together only in a small number of upper-middle-class areas (such as the Malone Road in south Belfast). While areas of Glasgow became somewhat 'Green' or 'Orange' following the immigration and settlement of both Irish Catholics and Ulster Protestants, no districts were dominated by one or the other. Protestant strongholds such as Bridgeton were partly mixed, as were the Irish Catholic enclaves such as Garngad. By 1914 over 700,000 people were living in Glasgow's three central square miles, the densest concentration of population in the whole of Europe.[50] Such lack of space was an obvious constraint on the creation of the rival ethnic ghettos that emerged in Liverpool and the Lancashire mill towns. Glasgow Corporation assumed control of working-class housing during the 1920s and for the next four decades cleared the slums, rebuilt the inner city and constructed large peripheral housing schemes. The Catholic- and Labour-dominated council had no reason to separate Catholics and Protestants in the shift of population.[51] In Belfast and Londonderry, on the other hand, control over housing allocation was a key pillar of Unionist power; housing segregation maintained predictable electoral outcomes. The outbreak of the Troubles in the late 1960s sharpened segregation in Northern Ireland as many Catholic and Protestant families were forced to flee back into traditional strongholds of towns, villages or particular housing estates.

The 2001 census allows us to compare, for the first time, segregation in Glasgow and Belfast. Catholics make up 29 per cent of the population of Glasgow. In no council ward do they form a majority, although they come close in Toryglen (45 per cent) and Hutchesontown (43 per cent). The commonly held view that Garngad remains a very Catholic part of Glasgow is not supported by the data; for every Catholic living in the Royston ward (approximating to the old Garngad district) there are two non-Catholics. On the other hand, the supposedly Protestant strongholds of Bridgeton and Govan are, in fact, both 30 per cent Catholic. The area with the smallest proportion of Catholics (12 per cent) is Pollokshields East, which also has the largest ethnic minority population in Scotland: four in ten residents are Muslim. In short, there is no obvious geographical pattern to Catholic residency in Glasgow.

In Belfast, 42 per cent of the population is Catholic. However, eleven council wards contain at least twice this figure, with five being at least 90 per cent Catholic. At the other extreme, Catholics form less than 3 per cent of the population in thirteen wards. The highly Catholic wards are generally situated in the west of the city and the highly Protestant wards situated in the east. However, some hugely contrasting areas sit side by side in more central and northern parts of Belfast; both New Lodge (93 per cent Catholic) and Falls (86 per cent Catholic) neighbour Shankill (less than 1 per cent Catholic), while Ardoyne (86 per cent Catholic) borders Crumlin (less than 2 per cent Catholic). If Catholics were to be equally spread across Belfast, then 40 per cent of the Catholic population would need to be relocated. The corresponding figure for Glasgow is only 11 per cent.[52] In the household survey of 2002, less than 7 per cent of Glaswegians felt that their religion had a bearing on where they could live and only 5 per cent said they would avoid a particular part of the city for the same reason. In brief, Belfast is segregated; Glasgow is not.

INTERMARRIAGE

The extent to which two populations intermarry is important both as a symptom and as a cause of integration. It is a symptom because the willingness to marry someone of another race, nation, ethic group or religion shows the importance of those characteristics as against personal emotional attachment. Because we can marry only those we meet, intermarriage also indicates the extent of mixing as equals. But it is also a cause of further integration. For bigots to maintain a culture or a structure of discrimination, they must be able to divide those they wish to advance ('oor ain folk') from those they wish to deprive of opportunities ('them'). The more that we marry them and produce children who cannot easily be labelled, the harder it is to discriminate and the more likely it is that religious or ethnic preferences will be over-ridden by other considerations. As populations mix, being a good uncle or brother-in-law competes with being a loyal Catholic or Protestant, and, in stable affluent societies that are not divided by competing political agendas, family trumps loyalty to religio-ethnic group.[53]

What do our two surveys tell us about intermarriage? First, they tell us that the vast majority of Scots have no objection to a relative marrying someone of a different religion. Across Scotland, only 3 per cent minded 'a great deal'; a further 7 per cent minded 'slightly'. Over two-thirds did not mind at all. There were no significant differences between the expressed views of Protestants and Catholics, irrespective of age. The same pattern was found in Glasgow, where only 3 per cent minded a great deal and over 80 per cent did not mind at all. Around a third of those in Glasgow who minded a great deal about mixed marriages were Muslim; a great over-representation. Catholics in Glasgow express, marginally, more tolerant views than Protestants. In turn, Protestants in Glasgow express more tolerant views than both Catholics and Protestants in Scotland as a whole.

The sentiment expressed in answers to the hypothetical survey question is matched by action. Put simply, it was once the norm for Catholics to marry other Catholics.[54] In our Scottish survey, almost all the married Catholics aged 65–74 (94 per cent to be precise) were married to a Catholic. The corresponding figure in the Glasgow study was 80 per cent. For Scotland as a whole the figure for those aged 55–64 was 86 per cent (69 per cent in Glasgow) and it gradually goes down for each age cohort until, for those aged 25–34, more than half the Catholics are married to non-Catholics. For Glasgow, over 40 per cent of married Catholics have non-Catholic spouses. To put these figures in context, we can note that in Northern Ireland in 1991 only 2 per cent of marriages were religiously mixed and in the USA in 1999 only 3 per cent of marriages were racially mixed.[55]

The point is compelling and simple. Young Scots no longer regard religion (or more precisely religio-ethnic identity) as an important consideration in the most important personal decision they make. This relative indifference to religion also shows up in socialising patterns. In the Glasgow survey only 6 per cent said that religion was a factor in whom they could have as a friend and that response was much more common from Muslim respondents than from Catholics or Protestants.[56]

SENSE OF NATIONAL AND CULTURAL IDENTITY

Joseph Bradley has suggested that, although the main objective differences between the heirs to the Irish and other Scots have been largely eroded, there is still a degree of cultural exclusion that has caused Scots Catholics of Irish descent to discover a renewed or entirely new interest in 'Irishness' as a distinct cultural identity.[57]

Catholics of Irish decent in Scotland do have the opportunity to express a wholly or partial Irish identity through sporting, cultural or political organisations including the Celtic Football Club, the Gaelic Athletic Association, the Ancient Order of Hibernians and, for the more radical, the James Connolly Society. By far the most popular outlet for the expression of Irish identity is through support for Celtic FC. In the Glasgow survey, we find that 74 per cent of respondents who support Celtic are Catholic. However, we must immediately qualify that by saying that almost half of those surveyed do not follow any football team.

But, where we find strong Catholic support for Celtic in these data, we do not find evidence in the Glasgow survey that Scots Catholics think of themselves as Irish. The survey allowed respondents to choose as many national or ethnic identities that they felt best represented them, and, while 81 per cent of Catholics chose Scottish and 23 per cent chose British, only 8 per cent chose an Irish identity. Furthermore, only one Catholic respondent claimed to be 'Irish-Scots'. When we put Bradley's claim at its most plausible, by analysing only Catholics who support Celtic, we find the proportion claiming an Irish identity remains at 8 per cent, the same as for Catholics who don't support a football team. A further investigation of those Catholics committed to Celtic by attending their matches 'nearly every week' shows that only two from twelve chose an Irish identity. We will return to football in Chapter 4.

Bradley's claims fare no better with data from the all-Scotland survey. As Table A3.6 shows, Catholics are more likely than Church of Scotland identifiers or people who claimed no religion to describe themselves as 'Scottish not British'. In both 1999 and 2001 Catholics were less likely than Church of Scotland identifiers to describe themselves as 'Equally Scottish and British' but in this they were no different from those people who claimed no religious identity. What is crucial is the 'other description' row in the table. The surveys allowed respondents to claim another identity. It was thus open to those who felt Irish rather than Scottish or British to say that. They did not.[58]

In an effort to provide the evidence to support their views, scholars such as Bradley and Mary Hickman encouraged those of

Irish descent in Scotland and England to record their identity as 'Irish' in the 2001 census. Adverts were taken out in places such as the *Irish Post* (a London-based paper) and *Celtic View*. The campaign did not produce the desired effect. The number of people resident in Scotland at the time of the census who chose to describe themselves as Irish (40,000) was less than the number of people who had been born in Ireland (55,000). That is, they were not Scots Catholics reacting to their oppressive environment by thinking of themselves as Irish. They were simply Irish in the sense that the people who said they were Swedes were Swedish.

Even before the census, a convenient explanation for this failure of reality was being composed. It was asserted that 'people born in Scotland with Irish parents or grandparents frequently hide their roots because they fear hostility' and hence 'the "Irish" box will not be fully used by those who feel they have an Irish cultural background'.[59] This seems implausible. When survey respondents are quite happy to declare their income, views about abortion, religious upbringing and attitudes to capital punishment, it is not likely that they become coy over ethnic identity.

Another place we might find evidence of Catholic alienation is in attitudes towards devolution. Although surveys provide little evidence for this, some commentators supposed that there was some reluctance among Catholics to support devolution during the 1970s campaigns because they feared that an autonomous Scotland would be a more unpleasantly Protestant country than one run from London.[60] In the run-up to the referendum on the Scottish Parliament, the late Cardinal Winning announced very publicly that Catholics had nothing to fear from a Scottish parliament. Whether he led or merely represented a change is not clear, but the voting suggests no Catholic hostility: 62 per cent were in favour. Of those who did vote, Catholics were as likely as Protestants to vote for a parliament, and also less likely than Protestants to have voted against.

The question of common identity was addressed head-on in the Glasgow survey. Respondents were asked how closely they identified with people of the same religious backgroun:, 44 per cent chose 'fairly close' or 'very close'. That might seem impressive until we note that respondents were more likely to identify with people of the same social-class background (61 per cent), people of the same race

(57 per cent), people brought up in the same area as them (56 per cent) and people living in their current neighbourhood (56 per cent). And remember that we know from the census data that neighbourhoods are not religiously homogenous. So, while religion is a fairly important source of communal identity in Glasgow, there are clearly more popular sources.[61]

DISTINCT POLITICS

It is typical of deeply divided societies that religio-ethnic groups pursue competing politics, either to further their own interests as a 'bloc' or to promote the interests of members of the religio-ethnic bloc in another state. When the Irish first moved to Scotland in significant numbers, they exhibited both patterns. Irish politics were repeated in a minor key in Scotland. There were branches of various Irish parties active in central Scotland, but once the Irish problem has been resolved with the formation of the Irish Free State in the early 1920s, the Irish in Scotland turned to local issues. Unlike the model of continental Europe, where Catholics formed sectional, often clergy-led, parties that were antithetical to the left, Scotland's Catholics became involved through the trade unions in the organisations that became the Labour party. Once the labour movement had conceded the main Catholic Church demand – control over its own schools – and once it had to come clear that Scottish labourism was neither communist nor particularly socialist, the Catholic Church dropped its opposition.

There has long been a strong ideological connection between Protestantism and unionism, meaning in this context support for the union of England and Scotland as the centre of the British Empire. That connection was strengthened when Gladstone's support for Irish home rule split the Liberal party and moved Liberal unionists into the 'Conservative and Unionist' party. For the first part of the twentieth century religious and political identities tended to overlap: Catholics were pro-Labour and anti-Conservative and Protestants were more likely to vote Conservative. A simple way of expressing the connection is to say that significant numbers of Catholics and Protestants voted against what elsewhere would have been their class interests: many working-class Protestants voted Conservative and many middle-class Catholics voted Labour.

Does this pattern still hold? Table A3.7 shows that Catholics do have a distinctly strong preference for Labour.[62] They are over-whelmingly Labour voters. More importantly, they remain so when we control for social class: in the Scottish survey 50 per cent of middle-class Catholics respondents said they voted for Labour. They are less likely than Protestants to support the Scottish Nationalists or, come to that, the Liberal Democrats and are even more distinctive in their hostility to the Conservatives: almost none voted Conservative. Looked at from the other end, although current levels of support are low, Scottish Protestants remain much more likely than others to vote Conservative.

In these calculations, we have identified respondents simply by the religious label they selected. We repeated the analysis for only those who attended church regularly. Church going Catholics are much more likely to vote Labour (65 per cent) than nominal Catholics and nominal and churchgoing Protestants (35, 36 and 37 per cent, respectively). And churchgoing Catholics are distinctive in their support for Labour irrespective of their class background. On the other side of the divide, it is middle-class churchgoing Protestants who are distinctive in their support for the Conservative party in Scotland (but still only 23 per cent).

This much continues the patterns of the past. However, a new pattern is revealed once we divide the sample into three age bands (see Table A3.8).[63] There is a marked decline in Labour support among younger Catholics (from more than two in three of older Catholics to less than one in three). In addition, the class divides of the past seem also to have disappeared among young Scots: they are now only really evident among older non-Catholic Scots. Put simply, only for an older generation of Scots do traditional class and religious loyalties still matter; for a younger generation they do not. In the 2001 general election, the most popular choice of Scots under the age of 35, irrespective of class or religion, was to abstain. In that light, talk about continuing Catholic support for Labour is irrelevant.

If we consider only the choices of those who did vote, we find some continuity with the past: younger churchgoing Catholics do vote (three-quarters voted in 2001) and they vote Labour (two-thirds of those who voted chose Labour). On the other side of the divide, the Conservative party is more popular with younger churchgoing Protestants than with other younger Scots. Thus, religion and politics continue to be intertwined, but, even so, the reach of religion has been so diminished in Scottish life, and also the political landscape and even what is understood to count as politics has so changed for a younger generation, that the same general conclusion can be drawn: for most younger Scots religion does not drive political preferences (and apparently, for many, the political process in Westminster does not matter anyway).

One might carelessly suppose that any sign of difference between Catholics and Protestants is evidence of a divided society. The matter is more complicated. When we compare Catholic and Protestant voting in Northern Ireland, we see two radically separated populations pulling in competing directions. In Scottish politics, Catholic distinctiveness is not in that sense divisive. Catholics are unusual only in being more likely than other Scots to support the political party that most Scots support. Labour is the preferred option of all Scots who vote. It is also the preferred party of Protestant Scots taken as a bloc: almost half of those Protestants who voted chose Labour, more than twice the number who voted for the next most popular choice. The minority Catholic population is not un-Scottish; it is hyper-Scottish. It is not Catholics who are unusual: it is that very small number of traditional Scottish Protestants who vote Conservative.

MORAL AND ETHICAL VALUES

The reach of religion in modern societies is typically short: even committed churchgoers expect it to instruct them only about their personal lives and not about their place in the economy or their politics. The one topic where we might expect to find major differences between Protestants and Catholics is sex.

Scots hold generally liberal views about sex before marriage: two-thirds think it is not wrong at all (see Table A3.9). The majority think that homosexuality should be explained to teenagers by teachers in school. Few think that abortion is wrong in every circumstance. Homosexuality polarises Scots and a majority of Scots think adultery is wrong. But when we explore what else distinguishes those who differ in their responses to these items, as we do with Table 3.5, we find that age is important but religion is not.

Table 3.5 Views on homosexuality by religion and age, Scotland, 2001 (%)

Age group	Percentage of each group who think homosexuality is always wrong			
	Roman Catholic	Protestant	No religion	Other religion
18–34 years	19	12	17	15
35–54 years	34	36	31	30
55+ years	62	61	58	38

Source: Scottish Social Attitudes survey (self-complete supplement N = 1,398).

Most of the older generation think homosexuality is wrong. Among the middle cohort, who grew up in the 1950s, 1960s and 1970s, it is only churchgoing Christians who are less likely to approve (but they are no more likely than other middle-aged Scots to disapprove). For the youngest cohort homosexuality is not wrong. Despite the positions taken by the church hierarchy, the effect of religion is weak even for Catholics. It is only with two very small populations that religion makes a big difference: churchgoing conservative Protestants and non-Christians.

Religion has more effect in shaping attitudes to sex education in schools. The secular middle classes are most likely to support teachers explaining homosexuality (fewer than one in ten think it wrong) and the secular working classes are correspondingly less supportive (but only about one in five think it wrong). It is older Catholics who stand out as least supportive: almost half disapprove.[64]

Religion also influences views on abortion, as do age and class. In general, only a minority of Scots think abortion is wrong almost always, but older Catholic respondents are much more likely to feel that: two-thirds think it wrong.[65] More than half of older working-class churchgoers disapprove, particularly those older Catholics who go regularly to mass.[66] Older churchgoers are the most disapproving, but there is little to choose between different religions. At well over 90 per cent, most churchgoers simply see adultery as wrong in almost all circumstances.

In sum, religion is an influence on socio-moral values but it matters much less to the young than to the old and on most topics religion is less important than age, class or education. That is, religion no longer determines this part of our culture. Only elderly churchgoing Catholics conform to the Church's conservative teachings. Otherwise there are not big differences between Catholics and mainstream Protestants. The great divide is not between Catholics and Protestants but between the Christian mainstream and the small number of evangelical Protestants and non-Christians.

Clive Field has summarised the conclusions of thirty years of opinion polls that concern religion in Scotland. His remarks on Catholic attitudes to moral values are worth repeating: 'the positions taken by Catholics and non-Catholics on these issues are not radically different . . . the statistics [show] a widening gulf between the leadership and teachings of the Catholic Church and people of all persuasions – Catholic and non-Catholic alike.'[67]

CLAIMS OF THE CHURCH

It is remarkable that commentators such as Bradley make much of the place of football in Catholic communal identity but overlook the Church. Two English academics have written: 'For the Catholic/ Irish community, Celtic are the greatest single ethno-cultural focus because they provide the social setting and process through which the community's sense of its own identity and difference from the indigenous community is sustained, in and through a set of symbolic processes and representations.'[68] When only three-quarters of Celtic supporters are Catholics and when mass attendance outnumbers Celtic Park attendance by a factor of 4, something is being missed.

We will shortly consider changes in rates of church involvement but first we want to consider the image that the Catholic Church has of itself. This is important, because too often the cohesion of the Catholic community (if such a term be appropriate) is treated as if it was primarily a consequence of external hostility. That the vast majority of Catholics in the 1920s married other Catholics, for example, is treated as a reflection of native Scots' unwillingness to accept the Irish and their descendants as social equals.

We should not rule out the possibility that much of the relative isolation of the Scots Catholic community derives from the Church's self-image and its disdain for other churches. Since the Reformation the Vatican has insisted that it possesses the only Christian faith and that all Protestant churches are false guides. Although militant Protestants were wildly wrong in their estimation of the power and influence of the Catholic Church, there was nothing wrong with their description of Catholicism as a faith that claimed unique access to the mind of God. In 1927 the leading English Catholic Fr Ronald Knox said: 'a body of Catholic patriots, entrusted with the government of a Catholic state, will not shrink even from repressive measures, in order to perpetuate the secure domination of Catholic principles among their fellow-countrymen.' More telling, he made it clear that the Church's support for liberal democracy was opportunistic: 'For when we demand liberty in the modern state, we are appealing to its own principles, not to ours.'[69] As late as the 1950s the Catholic Church still maintained officially that it had a right to impose its will on non-believers; the American Jesuit theologian John Courtney Murray was disciplined for suggesting that this was unacceptable in a democracy.

The Second Vatican Council of the early 1960s represented a major shift in Church thinking. Obstacles to mixed marriages were weakened in the 1980s, as was the insistence that the children of such unions be raised as Catholics. However, some priests still insist that they will not accept for First Communion children who do not attend a Catholic school. And in Vatican eyes Protestants have moved from 'heretics' only as far as 'our separated brethren'. The most potent sign of that separation is that the Church does not permit Protestants to take communion. Since 1971 members of all the major Scottish churches have collaborated in a pilgrimage to St Mary's Church, Haddington. The Protestants share communion at a single altar and the Church of Scotland gave permission for the Catholics to conduct a mass in the church. The officiating priests for many years turned a blind eye to the fact that many Protestants were stretching the limits of ecumenical cooperation by taking communion at the Catholic mass. In 1998 Archbishop Keith O'Brien wrote to the pilgrimage organisers telling them that this had to stop.

The gradual improvement in relations with other Christian churches has not changed the Catholic Church's fundamental belief that it is superior. At a dinner in Glasgow's City Halls to celebrate the fiftieth anniversary of his entry to the priesthood, Cardinal Winning said that Catholicism would be Scotland's sole faith in the twenty-first century. He said the papacy was willing to cede control of Scottish Catholicism in the cause of ecumenical unity but that such unity required that the Protestant churches admit they were wrong:

> The other churches will have to accept Bishops. There will be no movement on doctrine and no movement on the seven sacraments . . . When we speak to other churches, we have the right to say to them, 'Look right back to the beginning and ask yourselves, why did you abandon us?'[70]

The official position was given in 2001 by the Church's parliamentary officer in a letter to the *Herald*:

> The Catholic Church takes the position that Christ did entrust authority to the church, with one person given a special position of authority as described in Matthew's gospel . . . Christ also gave authority to the church to teach and the promise that the church would maintain the faith.[71]

It is clear that this disdain for other Christian organisations is not a function of persecution. It is the posture historically maintained by the Vatican even in places where it has an unchallenged monopoly.

In Scotland this matters little now because the Church is rapidly losing its people. The Scottish survey showed considerable fallout in religious identification (see Table A3.1). Of those who were raised as Catholics, 20 per cent now describe themselves as having 'no religion'. The decline of the Catholic Church began later than that of the Church of Scotland but it is now rapidly catching up. Mass attendance peaked in the 1950s at around 420,000. It then remained relatively stable until the early 1970s, when it began to fall rapidly.[72] Peter Brierley's regular (and reliable) church censuses show that between 1984 and 2002 Church of Scotland attendance fell from 361,340 to 228,500: a drop of 37 per cent. Over the same period, the Catholic Church recorded a drop of 42 per cent: from 345,950 to 202,110.[73] Another mark of institutional decay is difficulty in recruiting to the priesthood. In 1976 there were 193 men in training. In 1996 it was only 57.

Not only are fewer Scots who were raised as Catholics conforming to the church of their parents; those who do still attend are increasingly selective about which of the Church's teachings they will accept. An obvious case in point is the Church's teachings on contraception. That the typical Catholic family is of the same size as the non-Catholic family tells its own story about responses to the Church's ban on artificial contraception. In one part of the Scottish survey we asked if people agreed with church leaders speaking out on a variety of issues. The general pattern was clear: people were much more sympathetic to church leaders badgering the government about big issues such as world poverty than they were to the churches telling them what to do in their private lives. Although regular churchgoers were overall more sympathetic than those Scots who did not attend church, their rank ordering of issues was the same, which rather suggests that the Catholic Church's strong interest in controlling sexuality may not be that popular even with its core people. Almost all regular mass-going Catholics (93 per cent) think it is 'generally right' for church leaders to 'speak out about poverty'. For education the figure is 77 per cent; for abortion 73 per cent; and for the environment it is 68 per cent. But only 65 per cent of regular Catholic churchgoers think it is right for their church leaders to speak out about personal sexuality. Or, to put it the other way round, almost 10 per cent declined to choose and just over a quarter of committed Catholic church adherents thought it 'generally wrong' for the hierarchy to pronounce on sexuality.

The general background to the Catholic Church's loss of its people is the general secularisation of western Europe, which we have discussed at great length elsewhere.[74] But there is one interesting aspect of that secularisation that we would like to consider here and we can introduce it by raising the question of the effectiveness of Catholic schools. That the Catholic Church is now declining at the same rate as the Church of Scotland suggests that Catholic schools are failing in their primary task: to socialise the next generation in the faith. In part this is simply because the external secularising forces (such as the increasing diversity of our culture, increasing unwillingness to accept authority and increasing individualism) are becoming stronger: it has become harder to defend the faith. But there is a specific connection between schooling, church adherence and marrying 'out' that we would like to explore.

THE CHURCH—SCHOOL—FAMILY TRIANGLE

Historians disagree about the extent to which Irish Catholic migrants and their immediate descendants formed a closed community. We do not need to settle that argument; we need only note that declining rates of church adherence and increasing intermarriage with non-Catholics show community cohesion declining, irrespective of how high we set the starting point.

Part of the explanation of that change may be found in one corner of the church–school–family triangle. The main reason for involvement in the life of a church is belief in its tenets, but the family is an encouragement to such involvement. The ceremonies of family life – weddings, christenings, first communions – provide occasions for reaffirming one's ties. For those who have a faith, wanting to see their children raised in it is a good reason for active participation. The Catholic Church's schools have always provided a strong link between the Catholic family and the institutional church. In 1982, when the government issued a Parent's Charter promoting the right of parents to choose their children's school, Cardinal Winning responded with a pastoral letter, read out from all pulpits, reminding Catholics that they had a religious obligation to send their children to a Catholic school.

Discussions of the community-building (or, if you prefer, socially divisive) effects of Catholic schools usually concentrate on the friendship patterns of children. We would like to draw attention to the less obvious matter of the part that the school plays in the social world of parents. The accidental relations that develop around the school (through attending fund-raising events, waiting outside the school gate with the other parents, sharing lifts, helping with school trips, meeting the parents of children's friends) are often a major part of the social world of adults. Schools shape the social lives of parents as much as of pupils.

But this effect is confined to those adults who have school-age children and the number of children has fallen markedly. One way of describing fertility is to express the number of children born as a percentage of the number that women of child-bearing age could have had if they had been inhibited only by being pregnant: 'even when the high rates of illegitimate fertility are taken into account, only some 14.4 per cent of Scots women's potential fertility was being realised by 1988, compared with 19.2 per cent in 1931 and 26 per cent in 1911'.[75] This markedly reduces the number of adults linked to schools through their children. All Scottish adults will have been influenced by their own schooling but an ever-growing percentage will not have had that experience reinforced and continued by having their adult relationships shaped by their own children's schooling.

A related change that should have borne more heavily on Scottish

Catholics than non-Catholics is the decline in the typical family size. A woman who has five children at eighteen-month intervals will have children in school (assuming they typically start at 5 and leave at 16) for two decades. A woman who has only one child will be involved in schooling for only half that time. Thus, as the typical family shrinks, so does the social impact of schooling. National data from 1911 show that 'women married between the ages of 22 and 26 and living with their husbands for at least fifteen years had on average almost six children. More than one fifth had nine or more.'[76] The 1971 census data show that women who married between the ages of 22 and 24 in the mid-1940s had a mean family size of around 2.5 children. More than half had one or two.

Although the links between age of marriage, prevalence of marriage, number of children and lifespan are complex, the basic point can be extracted from the following:

> In 1900, Scottish working-class women would have spent around a third of their lives . . . producing, nursing and nurturing children up to the age of ten . . . By the early 1990s, with the average number of children per family at two and life expectancy up to seventy-seven years, this maternal care period had contracted to constitute about fifteen per cent of a woman's life span.[77]

If we add the years from 10 to 15 onto those figures to cover the rest of formal schooling, the effect of the change to smaller families would be stronger.

To see the relevance of the point, we can divide social relationships in two spheres: those based around the extended family and those of the public world of work. Most work settings typically involve mixing on equal terms with large numbers of people from different backgrounds. The private family world is built around inherited personal preferences and hence its relationships are more likely to reflect and reinforce those preferences. The more of our relationships that are derived from our families, the more likely we are to recreate our distinctive cultures. Or, to put it the other way round, the more time people spend away from the family and the home, the more likely they are to form friendships with people who do not share their religious and cultural background. The decline in fertility rates over the twentieth century reduces the role of the family and the school as a source of friends and acquaintances.

Not surprisingly, the shrinking of the family has been accompanied by a rise in the numbers of mothers who work outside the home. Between 1901 and 1931 the proportion of women in work changed little and was about 35 per cent. After the Second World War it rose rapidly, so that by 1991 it was 67 per cent.

SUMMARY

That people share a sense of identity is not itself proof that they are the victims of discrimination. Members of the Exclusive Brethren, a small evangelical Protestant sect, separate themselves from their host society from choice: the better to maintain their purity. Nonetheless there is commonly some causal connection between separation and discrimination: that they find themselves devalued and snubbed is one good reason why people turn in on themselves. In thinking about the social identity of Scots Catholics, it is not easy to weigh the relative power of the wishes of some Catholics to remain apart and the wishes of some Protestants to prevent integration. There is certainly evidence of the former: for example, the 1907 *Ne Temere* papal decree on the unacceptability of mixed marriage was intended by the Catholic Church to counter tendencies to integration. But we can bypass much of that argument by simply noting that, however much Catholics may once have formed a distinctive community, they do not do so now. And, to return to the main theme of this study, while separation, because it may in part be self-willed, does not of itself prove discrimination, the lack of it certainly weakens the case that modern Scotland is endemically sectarian. In Northern Ireland the terms 'Protestant' and 'Catholic' designate two largely separated and in many respects different peoples. That is not the case in Scotland.

Enduring Bigotry
In this final section we will try to assess the popularity and salience of anti-Catholicism. Many of the things that could be said under this heading have already been covered by implication in earlier parts of the chapter. The survey data on intermarriage, for example, can be taken as an index of Protestant attitudes towards Catholics as can the discussion of the public standing of the Catholic Church. Here we will consider some fields not previously addressed directly.

PUBLIC UTTERANCE

It is hardly controversial to say that anti-Catholic attitudes are very
rarely expressed in public life. In 1982 Billy Wolfe, one of the senior
figures in the SNP, resigned and left public life because he disapproved of the Pope's impending visit and he knew that such an
attitude would damage the party electorally.[78] In 1986 Councillor
Sam Campbell of Midlothian District Council was forced to resign
his council positions and was banished from the Labour party group
for two years after he made anti-Catholic remarks at an Orange rally
in Edinburgh. To rehabilitate himself he had to sign a formal
recantation. Councillor Thomas O'Dea of Falkirk Council made
the papers in 1996 when he was expelled from a British Legion Club
for drunkenness and singing sectarian songs.[79] When a video of
Donald Findlay QC, vice-chairman of Rangers Football Club,
singing Orange songs was leaked to the press, he was forced to
resign from the club, was sacked as Rector of St Andrews University
and was fined £3,000 (a relatively small sum for an advocate but a
profound humiliation) by the Faculty of Advocates. A more humble
case is equally telling: in 1998 a young Glasgow factory-worker was
sacked from her job for scribbling sectarian slogans on blank time-
sheets.[80] Clearly, sectarian views are no longer acceptable in Scottish
public life.[81]

THE ORANGE ORDER

The fact that the Orange Order still exists is often cited as evidence of
sectarianism. Its members would deny that it is a sectarian organisation and argue that its positive embodiment of Protestant virtues can
be separated from unpleasantness towards Catholics. Either way,
comparison of the Order in Scotland and in Northern Ireland, and of
the current Order and that of the early twentieth century, will tell us
something about the popularity of a set of beliefs and attitudes that
can support anti-Catholicism. The Order is much smaller in Scotland
than in Northern Ireland, it is confined to one small part of Scotland,
it is smaller than it was and it has no public influence.

At the turn of the century, the Loyal Orange Institution had
25,000 members in Scotland. At the same time it commanded
100,000 in Ulster, which had one-third of Scotland's population.
By 1914 the Order was four times as large in Canada as in Scotland
but the population was less than twice as large.[82] Membership in

Scotland rose during the Irish home-rule crisis and again following the outbreak of the Troubles in 1969. Estimations of its current membership range from 50,000 to 80,000 (with the lower end more plausible) out of a population of over four million non-Catholics. Attendance at the parades themselves appears to have declined. While 40,000 could be mustered during the 1970s, the figure for the main parade of 1999 at Drumpellier Park, Coatbridge, was estimated at 20,000.[83] The same weekend, 80,000 people attended an open-air pop concert.

Unlike the Order in Northern Ireland, the Scottish Institution has no formal say in the policies of the Conservative party and, unlike the situation in the 1930s, there is no overlap of personnel. No senior Tory politicians are members of the Grand Lodge; indeed, as far as we can discover, no politician of any consequence is a member of the Order. Orangeism so lacks political clout that Orange parades are frequently banned by local councils. Despite being dominated by Conservatives and Nationalists (not the obvious enemies of Orangeism), Perth and Kinross Council in 1986 banned a parade of what a councillor called a sectarian organisation. In 2000 Forfar banned a march. The 2001 Orange march in Aberdeen was the first in fourteen years and it only took place only after a sheriff had ruled that the council's ban on Orange parades was a disproportionate response to some trouble that had occurred at a march in 1987. Councillor George Urquhart said that the Orange Order would not be welcomed back to Aberdeen.[84] And it was a Tory member of the Scottish Parliament who in 2003 suggested that Orange marches should be banned because they damaged the incomes of local businesses.[85]

An important mark of the social standing of the Orange Order is its complete alienation from the national church. When a Forfar minister discovered that the Orange Lodge had been meeting in a hall that the Church of Scotland had forgotten it owned, he immediately ended the let to what he described as 'a religiously intolerant group'.[86] There are now no Scottish clergymen in its membership. The last Church of Scotland minister, Gordon McCracken, resigned in July 1998 in protest at the violence associated with the Order's Drumcree protests in Northern Ireland. The gradual disappearance of clergy support for the Order over the twentieth century is clear in the statistics presented in William

Marshall's *The Billy Boys*. There have been only five clergymen associated with the Order in Scotland since the 1940s. That is not a misprint. The Orange Order, which is often cited as proof of Scottish anti-Catholicism, has had only five clergy supporters in sixty-five years.

The creation in 1999 of a Scottish parliament elected by proportional representation offered the ideal conditions for very small parties to gain some political presence and legitimacy. The Scottish Unionist party had first been floated in 1985 by Orangemen who felt that the Anglo-Irish agreement negotiated by Margaret Thatcher in that year was a betrayal of Ulster unionists. The winner-takes-all election system of local government and Westminster elections discouraged any candidates from standing until the first elections to the Scottish Parliament. Among its policy positions was opposition to 'apartheid schools'. It polled less than 1 per cent of the second vote in the three regional lists it contested.[87] Candidates also stood in some wards in local-government elections and did no better. The voters of Dennistoun, whose grandparents had elected Alexander Ratcliffe of the Scottish Protestant League in the 1930s, gave just seventy-five votes to the Scottish Unionist party.

ATTITUDES TO DENOMINATIONAL SCHOOLS

Opposition to state-funded Catholic education is often taken as a mark of bigotry. When First Minister Jack McConnell supported plans for closer ties between Catholic and non-denominational schools by creating shared campuses, Archbishop Mario Conti angrily responded that calls for the abolition, or even amalgamation, of Catholic schools were 'tantamount to asking for the repatriation of the Irish, and just as offensive'.[88] Conroy has argued that, because the original 1918 Education Act was opposed by bigots such as Alexander Ratcliffe, anyone who is at all critical of the state funding of Catholic schools must be inspired by the same sentiments.[89]

Before we consider the motives behind various forms of opposition to segregated education, it is worth considering the distribution of preferences. A large majority of Protestants has always been opposed to segregated schools, but in recent years Catholic attitudes have changed. In 1992 47 per cent of Catholics were in favour of phasing out separate schools. In 2001 the figure was 59 per cent.[90] In the Glasgow survey, those raised as Catholics generally think denominational schools are a 'good thing' and Protestants generally think the opposite. Support is stronger among older Catholics, whilst, among Protestants, the negative response does not vary much by age.[91] Younger Glaswegians (both Catholics and Protestants) were more likely than the older respondents to agree with the statement 'Catholic schools create intolerance', but the religious divide remains strong: about 40 per cent of Protestants felt separate schools created intolerance whilst 50 per cent of Catholics think they do not. Those who were raised with no religion are most opposed to segregated schools.

It is not easy to disentangle possible motives for preferring a single integrated system to a divided one. Clearly the 1920s opposition of people such as Alexander Ratcliffe was sectarian but most current unease seems based on quite different considerations. One such is the French idea that a single national system would more effectively sustain a coherent national identity. Another supposes that the modern state should not interfere in religion. As the US Constitution puts it: the state should neither hinder the free exercise of religion nor promote any religion. For the state to fund church schools (especially when it does not offer to fund schools for all faiths) is to give legitimacy to one particular religion. Especially when so few Scots are involved in the Catholic Church, state subsidies for its activities seems inappropriate. A third consideration is the belief that separate schools encourage sectarianism. One might argue that this case is so implausible that it could be made only by those who are inspired by anti-Catholic animus, but in the absence of any separate evidence for that we must suppose that organisations such as the National Secular Society[92] are sincere in thinking themselves to be even-handedly secular.

The Scottish survey shows that respondents raised without any religion are more opposed to the state funding of Catholic schools than the other respondents. This suggests that secular objections are more common than anti-Catholic ones.

Those who take any opposition to the wishes of the Catholic Church as proof that Scotland is endemically sectarian are often missing the bigger point that very few of those who wished for a single national system have pressed the matter. A clear majority of Labour party activists, educationalists and Scots generally (including in recent polls a majority of Catholics) are in favour of phasing out separate schools. Despite the concerns of many non-Catholic members that the system gives an unfair advantage to Catholic teachers (who can work in both sectors), the main teaching union, the Educational Institute of Scotland, did not discuss the issue for almost thirty years. That is resurfaced in 1998 was largely due to Cardinal Winning's suggestion that the Catholic system should be expanded, with the addition of Catholic nursery departments to existing primary schools.[93] If devolution was, in John Smith's sonorous phrase, the 'settled will of the Scottish people', then, by the same majorities, integration is the settled will of the Scottish people for education. But most Scots do not get excited about the matter. Far from being evidence of bigotry, the attitude to the state funding of religious schools seems to show commendable tolerance of a minority preference.

THE COLLAPSE OF CATEGORIES

An obvious difficulty for bigotry (which clearly plays a part in its decline) is the unpopularity of religion. When the vast majority of Scots have no particular religion and care not at all about theological disputes, criticisms of one group of people because they have the wrong religion clearly fall on deaf ears. Outside the tiny populations of conservative evangelical Protestants in the Highlands and Islands, there are now very few Scots who are at all interested in the status of the Vatican or the correct number of sacraments. The decline of conservative Protestantism means the end of 'religious' anti-Catholicism. In Chapter 2 we drew attention to the paucity of clergy support for militant Protestantism in the 1930s. As our remarks above about the absence of clergy in the Orange Order shows, religious legitimation is now entirely absent. Those who wish to regard the Catholic as an 'other' have to justify their actions on grounds other than religion and there are few of those. Scottish Catholics do not have a distinctive political agenda, do not have an unusual social class profile that can allow the ascription of social vices, and are not culturally distinctive. The social divisions needed to sustain sectarianism no longer exist, which explains why, in the Glasgow survey, most respondents who thought sectarianism a major problem had in mind football-related violence (of which more in the next chapter).

Conclusion

It is not easy to evaluate claims that Scotland is a sectarian country because those claims are usually formulated very loosely and shift promiscuously between assertions about discrimination, distinctiveness and dislike. Taking each separately, we have tried to clarify what is at issue and to find appropriate evidence. We reserve our explanation of the causal connections between the three fields until the final chapter. Here we summarise all the above as follows. We found little or no evidence of effective discrimination against Catholics. Our large-scale surveys showed little or no difference in socioeconomic status between young Catholics and non-Catholics. We also noted that, although churchgoing Catholics differ slightly from other Scots on a few matters of moral choice, they do not now (if they ever did) form a coherent subculture. Finally we have drawn attention to the weakness and unpopularity of anti-Catholicism.

Notes

1. By 1974 it was the choice of 24 per cent; see C. Field, "The haemorrhage of faith?": opinion polls as sources for religious practices, beliefs and attitudes in Scotland since the 1970s', *Journal of Contemporary Religion*, 16 (2001), pp. 157–75.

2. S. Bruce and T. Glendinning, 'Religious beliefs and differences', in C. Bromley, J. Curtice, K. Hinds and A. Park (eds), *Devolution – Scottish Answers to Scottish Questions* (Edinburgh: Edinburgh University Press, 2003), pp. 89–91.

3. It is worth adding that many European countries as late as the twentieth century required all citizens, or particularly prominent ones such as members of the government and civil service, to be members of the national church. See S. Bruce, *Politics and Religion* (Oxford: Polity Press, 2003), p. 171.

4. www.newadvent.org/cathen/13613a.htm

5. It also prevents illegitimate or adopted children becoming sovereign and favours male heirs. Although the act does not prevent members of the royal family from becoming or marrying Roman Catholics, it does remove them from the line of succession if they so do.

6. *Herald*, 3 July 2002.

7. *Herald*, 9 July 2002.

8. Montieth's obituary appeared in *Scottish Catholic Observer*, 24 December 1993, with no suggestion that he was unique or even unusual.

9. The background to this award was made public in early December 2003 when the minutes of the government committee that suggests names to the Queen for her honours list were leaked to the press. The decision had been made to recommend O'Neill and, for balance, the committee considered making a

similar award to someone associated with Glasgow Rangers. It could not think of anyone suitable. The important point for our concerns is the order in which the decisions were made.

10. J. McCaffrey, 'The Irish vote in Glasgow in the later nineteenth century', *Innes Review*, 21 (1970), pp. 30–6.
11. The Catholic Church's canon law would prevent any serving priest taking up a seat.
12. T. Gallagher, *Glasgow: The Uneasy Peace* (Manchester: Manchester University Press, 1987), pp. 142–3.
13. W. W. Knox, 'Religion and the Scottish labour movement *c.* 1900–39', *Journal of Contemporary History*, 23 (1988), pp. 609–30.
14. Gallagher, *Glasgow*, p. 272.
15. M. Keating, R. Levy, J. Geekie and J. Brand, 'Labour elites in Glasgow', *Strathclyde Papers on Government and Politics*, 61 (1989), p. 19.
16. L. Paterson, *Scottish Education in the Twentieth Century* (Edinburgh: Edinburgh University Press, 2003), p. 59.
17. J. Devine, 'A Lanarkshire perspective on bigotry in Scottish society', in T. Devine (ed.), *Scotland's Shame? Bigotry and Sectarianism in Modern Scotland* (Edinburgh: Mainstream, 2000), pp. 102–3.
18. Gallagher, *Glasgow*, p. 115.
19. L. Paterson, 'Salvation through education? The changing social status of Scottish Catholics', in Devine (ed.), *Scotland's Shame?,* pp. 145–57.
20. NFO Social Research, *Sectarianism in Glasgow – Final Report* (2003), p. 27.
21. The Housing Association Ombudsman for Scotland, *Investigation of a Complaint against Bridgeton and Dalmarnock Housing Association Ltd*, Ref: IR11/100/96, 10 November 1997. The events considered occurred in 1995.
22. According to the 2001 census, just over half of the population of Coatbridge is Catholic. Catholics also form 30 per cent of Airdrie's population.
23. For a detailed discussion of 'Monklandsgate', see G. Walker, *Intimate Strangers: Political and Cultural Interaction between Scotland and Ulster in Modern Times* (Edinburgh: John Donald, 1995), pp. 180–4.
24. Joe Carlen from the *Airdrie & Coatbridge Advertiser* interviewed on Radio Five's 'Two Tales of a City', 24 December 1995.
25. Data from 1979 Scottish election survey kindly provided by David McCrone.
26. J. Scott and J. Hughes, *The Anatomy of Scottish Capital* (London: Croom Helm, 1980), p. 200.
27. H. Conroy, 'Our schools must stay', *Scottish Catholic Observer*, 6 August 1999.
28. Paterson, 'Salvation through education?', pp. 151–3.
29. We recognise that reducing social class to manual versus non-manual is clumsy and loses a lot of analytical detail but it is necessary in order to retain sufficient numbers for comparisons of religion and age, and, even then, it ignores gender segmentation.
30. Valid chi-square tests show that the differences in the occupational position of older Protestants and Catholics are statistically significant ($P < 0.01$).
31. We do recognise that there is also significant disadvantage in rural areas of Scotland (e.g. Caithness and Sutherland).

32. The only group for which significant religious differences can be detected is among older men. Older Catholic men (age 55+) are in fact significantly less likely than their Protestant counterparts to consider such work discrimination to be commonplace. The test is at the margins of validity and it is worth noting the small number of older Catholic men available for analysis in the sample (N = 43).

33. We can only guess what these people had experienced but it may be that they are teachers disgruntled at the fact that jobs in Catholic schools are open only to Catholics.

34. P. Walls and R. Williams, 'Sectarianism at work: accounts of employment discrimination against Irish Catholics in Scotland', *Ethnic and Racial Studies*, 26 (2003), pp. 632–62. We have a general problem with the interviewers' method of simply inviting people to talk about discrimination without challenging them as to the adequacy of their knowledge or their reliance on hearsay. The only time the researchers challenge their respondents concerns the case of a Protestant who mentions the privileged position of Catholic teachers in regard to the Catholic school sector. Here they justify discrimination and say that the religious requirement relates only to the teaching of religious and moral education. They are wrong. The Catholic Church has the legal right to demand that all teachers in Catholic schools be Catholic, irrespective of subject.

35. Unison Scotland, 'Response to the cross-party working group report on religious hatred', February 2003, p. 3.

36. Gallagher, *Glasgow*, p. 251. O'Hagan also claims that Catholics are denied jobs in banks and insurance companies ('Into the ferment', in Devine (ed.), *Scotland's Shame?*, p. 27). Unfortunately he offers no source for evidence and apart from the Gallagher anecdote we cannot find any evidence that bears on this point.

37. *Herald*, 9 December 2002.

38. Gallagher, *Glasgow,* p. 246.

39. Ibid. p. 244.

40. J. C. Conroy, ' "Yet I live here": a reply to Bruce on Catholic education', *Oxford Review of Education*, 29 (2003), p. 406.

41. Small numbers prevent very detailed analysis but, in the division of the economically active respondents in the Scottish survey into self-employed, private sector, public sector and charity/voluntary sector, dichotomised into manual versus non-manual workers and those raised as Catholics versus others, the only statistically significant result suggests that, among middle-aged manual workers, those raised as Catholics are slightly more likely than others to work in the charity/voluntary sector (which itself is very small: only 2.2 per cent of the sample). For the 59 per cent in the private sector and 35 per in the public sector there is no discernible religion effect.

42. Gallagher, *Glasgow*, p. 273.

43. T. Gallagher, *Edinburgh Divided: John Cormack and No Popery in Edinburgh in the 1930s* (Edinburgh: Polygon, 1987), p. 187.

44. NFO Social Research, *Sectarianism in Glasgow – Final Report* (2003), pp. 26–7.

45. These figures were given in the following replies to written questions in the Scottish Parliament in 2001: S1W 15693, 15994, 14834 and 13187.

46. K. M. Wolfe, *The Churches and the British Broadcasting Corporation 1922–1956* (London: SCM Press, 1984), p. 79.

47. P. Lynch, 'The Catholic Church and political action in Scotland', in R. Boyle and P. Lynch, *Out of the Ghetto? The Catholic Community in Modern Scotland* (Edinburgh: John Donald, 1998), pp. 52–3.

48. There was a sizeable contingent from Ian Paisley's Free Presbyterian Church of Ulster.

49. H. Reid, *Outside Verdict: An Old Kirk in a New Scotland* (Edinburgh: Saint Andrew Press, 2002).

50. S. G. Checkland and O. Checkland, *Industry and Ethos: Scotland 1832–1914* (London: Edward Arnold, 1984).

51. I. Paterson, 'Sectarianism and municipal housing allocation in Glasgow', *Scottish Affairs*, 39 (2002), pp. 39–53.

52. This is calculated using the Index of Dissimilarity, which measures the amount of redistribution required in the hypothetical case that Catholics are equally represented in all council wards, having controlled for the existing Catholic population share in each ward.

53. Note the qualification that this assertion refers only to stable affluent societies. The atrocities that accompanied the break-up of the former Yugoslavia remind us that the replacement of large group loyalties by a combination of kinship bonds and universalism is not irreversible.

54. A variety of sources suggest that the marrying-out rate was higher in the nineteenth century. R. D. Lobban, 'The Irish community in Greenock in the nineteenth century', *Irish Geography*, 6 (1971), p. 279, says that 20 per cent of Irish Catholics in Greenock in 1851 married out. The underlying pattern is this: when there were relatively few Catholics in Scotland, Catholics married out because the alternative was to remain single. As the Catholic population grew, endogamy became possible and hence more common. It declined towards the end of the twentieth century as religion declined in significance. That is, the marriage patterns are explained by the complex movements of two factors: the availability of partners of the same religion and the importance of religion.

55. V. Morgan, M. Smith, G. Robinson and G. Fraser, *Mixed Marriages in Northern Ireland* (Coleraine: Centre for the Study of Conflict, University of Ulster, 1996).

56. The figures were 20 per cent of Muslims but only 4 per cent of Protestants and 6 per cent of Catholics.

57. J. Bradley, *Ethnic and Religious Identity in Modern Scotland: Culture, Politics and Football* (Aldershot: Avebury, 1995).

58. In this survey and two previous ones, respondents were asked a question that forced them to choose between British, English, European, Scottish, Irish, Northern Irish, Welsh and 'none of these'. Out of the 4,750 respondents to the three surveys, thirty (or less than 1 per cent) chose 'Irish' – a number so small it is likely that they were actually Irish people temporarily resident in Scotland rather than Scots making an ethnic point. We are grateful to David McCrone for supplying the data from the 1999, 2000 and 2001 Scottish Social Attitudes surveys.

59. E. Buie, 'Irish feel forced to hide roots', *Herald*, 11 April 2001. The story was based on quotations from Joseph Bradley. On the subject of hiding identity, it is worth reporting that in at least one case the fact that a secondary school was readily identifiable as Roman Catholic was due to the Catholic Church's preference. Because the local state secondary in Motherwell in the 1930s did not have the word 'Motherwell' in its name (it was Dalziel High School), the inspectors recorded the name of the then Higher Grade Catholic school simply as 'Motherwell Higher Grade School' on leaving certificates. The Director of Education asked for 'RC' to be included and the reply was that RC was used only when there was a chance of confusion. The director consulted the Church authorities, who came back with the suggestion of 'Our Lady's High School' and thus turned down a chance to allow their pupils to disguise their religion. We are grateful to Lindsay Paterson for this historical snippet.

60. On attitudes to Scots nationalism in the 1970s, see J. Kellas, *The Scottish Political System* (Cambridge: Cambridge University Press, 1975), pp. 116–42. On the 1930s, see J. Brand, *The National Movement in Scotland* (London: Routledge Kegan Paul, 1978), p. 213.

61. There are no significant differences when controlling for age.

62. Because we suppose that what matters for most of the concerns here is religious identity as a parallel with ethnic or national identity, we have used the claimed religious identities rather than some measure of religious practice to identify Catholics and Protestants. In the later section on socio-economic status we have used religion of upbringing to identify the groups because we expect that discrimination, if there is any, will be based on imputed rather than claimed identity.

63. We have performed this analysis just for Labour voting among Catholics because there are too few cases for meaningful analysis of all options and even when looking only at the Labour vote the sample numbers are small.

64. Conservative Protestants and non-Christians were also more likely to disapprove.

65. As to a lesser extent do middle-aged, middle-class Catholic men.

66. Again, the devout from minority churches are more likely to disapprove.

67. Field, ' "The haemorrhage of faith?" ', p. 166.

68. D. Burdsey and R. Chappell, ' "And if you know your history": an examination of the formation of football clubs in Scotland and their role in the construction of social identity', *Sports Historian*, 21 (May 2001); http://www2.umist.ac.uk/sport/SPORTS%HISTORY/sh211.html

69. Quoted in E. Campion, *Rockchoppers: Growing up Catholic in Australia* (Harmondsworth: Penguin, 1982), p. 26.

70. *Scotsman*, 16 January 1999. It might have been possible to view Winning's speech as the Catholic equivalent of Donald Findlay QC singing *The Sash*: an action intended to show membership of a community to other members of that community with the actual words spoken being merely 'form'. However, Winning repeated them for public consumption.

71. *Herald*, 27 January 2001.

72. P. Brierley, *Religious Trends No. 2, 2000–2001* (London: Christian Research, 1999), table 8.6.4.

73. P. Brierley, *Turning the Tide: The Challenge Ahead. Report of the 2002 Scottish Church Census* (London: Christian Research, 2003), pp. 16–17.

74. See e.g. S. Bruce, *God is Dead: Secularization in the West* (Oxford: Basil Blackwell, 2002) and *Religion in the Modern World: From Cathedrals to Cults* (Oxford: Oxford University Press, 1996).

75. M. Anderson, 'Population and family life', in T. Dickson and J. H. Treble (eds), *People and Society in Scotland*, vol. III *1914–1990* (Edinburgh: John Donald, 1992), p. 33.

76. Ibid. p. 36.

77. A. McIvor, 'Gender apartheid? Women in Scottish society', in T. M. Devine and R. J. Finlay (eds), *Scotland in the 20th Century* (Edinburgh: Edinburgh University Press, 1996), p. 191.

78. He later gave up Protestantism and became a New Ager; W. Wolfe, 'Forging a covenant with my conscience', *Herald*, 24 October 1992, pp. 12–13.

79. *Herald*, 21 May 1996.

80. *Herald*, 19 March 1998.

81. This story has an echo that shows how almost anything can be presented as evidence of anti-Catholicism. In 1989 Celtic sacked the editor of *Celtic View* when the *Sun* reported an inflammatory outburst of support for the IRA that he had made at a private meeting of football fanzine editors. Bradley presents this, not as evidence that the man in question uttered unacceptable sentiments or even that Celtic had behaved responsibly in sacking him, but as proof that the Scottish press is anti-Catholic; see J. Bradley, 'Facets of the Irish diaspora: "Irishness" in 20th century Scotland', *Irish Journal of Sociology*, 6 (1996), p. 89.

82. E. McFarland, *Protestants First: Orangeism in 19th Century Scotland* (Edinburgh: Edinburgh University Press, 1990), p. 106.

83. For the 1973 figure see S. Bruce, *No Pope of Rome: Militant Protestantism in Modern Scotland* (Edinburgh: Mainstream, 1985), p. 186. See *Sunday Herald*, 15 August 1999, for 1999 estimate.

84. *Press and Journal*, 24 September 2001.

85. *Orange Torch*, October 2003.

86. *Herald*, 5 May 2000.

87. The system of proportional representation used for the Scottish Parliament gave electors two votes. They voted for a candidate for their area in a first-past-the-post context; with the second vote they expressed a party preference. Those votes were used to create a measure of party preference. Candidates were then selected from the list of party candidates to top up the totals of those elected on the first vote so that for each region the overall number of elected members was representative of party preferences. Although people might have been reluctant to cast their first vote for people who had no chance of winning, they should have been less inhibited in the party preference vote. Hence we can take this tiny vote as indicative of support for the SUP.

88. *Herald,* 11 December 2002.

89. J. Conroy, 'A very Scottish affair: Catholic education and the state', *Oxford Review* of *Education*, 27 (2001), pp. 543–58.

90. 1992 figure comes from the Scottish Election Survey; the 2001 figure comes from the Scottish Social Attitudes survey.

91. Within that overall pattern of differences between Protestants and Catholics, middle-class and educated Protestants are the least positive about Catholic schools 'as a good thing' (only around 1 in 10 are supportive); among Glasgow Catholics, education level and class tend not to matter for support of Catholic schools (at between 40 and 50 per cent of differing social groups of Catholics).

92. National Secular Society, *Response to the Scottish National Debate on Education*, (London: National Secular Society, 2002).

93. *Herald*, 7 January 1998.

4 Ulster, Football and Violence

Introduction

On Saturday, 7 October 1995, Mark Scott, a young Celtic fan, and two friends left Celtic Park after watching their team play Partick Thistle. His route to the city centre took him through Bridgeton, along London Road. As Scott passed the Windsor Bar, one of a group of Rangers fans came up behind him and slashed his throat. He staggered some distance before collapsing and dying from loss of blood.

Scott's assailant was Jason Campbell, an unemployed van boy whose father and uncle had been leading figures in the Bridgeton cell of the loyalist paramilitary Ulster Volunteer Force (UVF). Colin and William 'Big Bill' Campbell had been convicted in 1973 of possessing explosives after a load of unstable mining gelignite they had been storing had exploded in the Apprentice Boys Hall in Landressy Street.[1] Not long after their release from prison, they and other members of their small group had tried to bomb two Glasgow pubs.[2] The Clelland Bar in the Gorbals was seriously damaged and ten people were slightly injured. The bomb at the Old Barns in Calton had not completely detonated and the damage was so slight that the customers carried on drinking. The UVF group had been under police surveillance for some time and convictions were easily obtained when a number of members decided to give evidence against the Campbells. Jason Campbell's defence lawyer was Donald Findlay QC, the vice-chairman of Glasgow Rangers Football Club, whose disgrace was described in the previous chapter. A year after Campbell had been convicted and sent to prison, he came back to public attention when, during peace negotiations in Northern Ireland, a UVF delegate to the talks tried to have him transferred to an Ulster prison – a move that would have resulted in him benefiting from the planned early release of political prisoners. This request was always a little strange in that the Campbells were not popular with most of the UVF's Belfast leadership and it may well have been an accidental by-product of the structure of the negotiations. Obviously the main purpose was to persuade the IRA to end its violence, but, in order to seem to be even-handed, the British government had to take the loyalist delegates seriously. One of the IRA demands was for its prisons in British prisoners to be 'repatriated'. Loyalist negotiators may have been encouraged into a 'me-too' strategy and, having no prisoners in Britain, fallen upon the name of Jason Campbell. Whatever the logic, when details of the request were leaked, there was such an outcry that the political spokesmen for the UVF denied that it had been approved by them and the matter was dropped.

In that small sad story we have a microcosm of what sectarianism now means to most people in Scotland: the Ulster conflict, football rivalry and street violence. Those are the subject of this chapter.

The Northern Ireland Troubles
Once the Irish problem had been temporarily solved with the creation of the Irish Free State and the devolved Stormont Parliament for Northern Ireland, Ireland dropped off the Scottish agenda. By the time it returned to the front pages of the Scottish newspapers in 1970, very few Scots were interested in the Orange and the Green. Despite the strong historical ties and kinship links, the Troubles had only feint echoes in Scotland.

Of course, there were rhetoric and posturing. In 1971, when it had seemed that Northern Ireland was on the brink of an all-out civil war, John Adam, the Grand Secretary of the Orange Order in Scotland, toured Orange halls and asked ex-servicemen and men with National Service or Territorial Army experience to volunteer to fight in Ulster. But the idea was dropped as quickly as it was raised and no one actually went. Very small numbers of working-class Protestants got involved in the loyalist paramilitary organisations, but their contribution to the war in Ulster was slight. Some weapons were collected and shipped to Ulster but they were often of very poor quality. The main purchase of one UVF cell, which led to them all being imprisoned, was of a fifty-year-old rusted-up revolver, which had been found on the beach at Dysart. The only time a Scottish group is known to have collected a large consignment of arms – when a young gun shop assistant murdered his manager and sold some seventeen rifles and handguns to the 'Supreme Commander' of the Ulster Defence Association (UDA) in Scotland – they never made it to Belfast. Instead they were transported ineptly around Scotland, sometimes by couriers who had to be coerced, before coming to lie in a damp cellar, where they stayed for sixteen months until all the handlers were lifted by the police. In all some thirty men were convicted for their part in a crime that was of no value at all to loyalists in Ulster.

What was useful in the early days before the loyalists developed international supply chains was the steady trickle of mining gelignite from the Scottish coalfields that found its way to Ulster. The typical career was of a UDA or UVF cell coming across a miner who either volunteered or was persuaded to steal four or five sticks at a time from the coalface. This would be accumulated and shipped to Belfast (in one interception, the police found 263 sticks of gelignite and 275 lbs of Sodium Chlorate, the basis for home-made explosives), where it was used with fatal consequences by loyalist paramilitaries. The only major terrorist incident in Scotland was the pub bombs mentioned above and it is clear from the testimonies given in court and from our interviews with some of the participants that, while men were willing to show solidarity with loyalists in Northern Ireland by fund raising, very few had any stomach for bringing Belfast's violence to Glasgow.

Such cases led to demands that the Orange Order clarify its position on terrorism. Orange Lodge Grand Secretary David Bryce, commenting on a series of severe sentences for weapons offences, said:

> The sentences will be a warning to other people who think there is something romantic about obtaining arms. We in the Orange

Order certainly do not condone violence nor do we condone the gathering of arms. There is no place in our organisation for people like those convicted or for anyone involved in paramilitary organisations.[3]

Very small groups of Orangemen periodically made militant noises. The papal visit of 1982 was the object of attention of one such grouping that called itself the Scottish Loyalists. At the time, a leading member told one of us: 'We have plans to stop this visit. We will smash the Mass. We will destroy the Pope's visit. We have told them this. If the police try to stop us, we will fight them. If the police want blood on the streets, we will give it to them.' The visit went ahead with no discernible disruption.

The Orange Order quickly developed a posture towards Northern Ireland that it has maintained steadfastly since. It supported the political line of the Ulster Unionist Party: nothing more. Any members convicted of serious crimes were expelled. When a local lodge refused to expel a member so convicted, Grand Lodge suspended its officers. In 1990 the Edinburgh 'Pride of Midlothian' Lodge had its warrant lifted for refusing to expel two members accused of fund raising for loyalist paramilitaries.

Legal but nonetheless provocative signs of support for paramilitary activity were more difficult to handle. Partly inspired by the politicisation of some republican flute bands, some young Protestants formed the Young Cowdenbeath Volunteers flute band and took as their uniforms and banners replicas of those of the 1914 14th battalion of the Royal Irish Rifles. At first hearing this sounds like just the sort of celebration of British military traditions that the Orange Order should approve. But there was a second meaning to these symbols. Before it enlisted in the British army, the 14th battalion had been the Young Citizens Volunteers, a corp of Sir Edward Carson's potentially rebellious 1912 UVF. The name had been revived in the 1970s by the youth wing of the current terrorist UVF. So by parading in replica uniforms, being Young, from Cowdenbeath, and Volunteering, the members of the YCV band managed to thumb their noses at the Orange leadership. At an Orange rally in Broxburn, West Lothian, Grand Master Magnus Bain ordered the YCV off the parade. For some time it looked as if dissent would fracture the Order, but in the end the vast majority of

members accepted the ban on gestures of support for Ulster paramilitary organisations. At the time of the Pride of Midlothian
dispute, there was talk of forming a breakaway Independent Orange
Order, but nothing came of it.

We cannot document this but we have a clear impression that,
since the 1994 ceasefires in Northern Ireland, the Scottish press has
made more of Scottish connections with the Ulster conflict.[4] When
the wife and children of notorious UDA gangster Johnny 'Mad Dog'
Adair fled from vengeful former colleagues in Belfast and arrived in
Scotland on the Stranraer ferry, the *Daily Record* ran the single word
INVASION full across its front page. There is little surprise that
some young men (and it is always men) who have family connections with Northern Ireland sometimes become involved. What is
much more noteworthy but rarely reported is that there is so little of
such involvement. We may have missed one or two cases, but our
records show only five cases of Scots being involved in Ulster-related
terrorist activities since 1995. Despite the strong family ties across a
short stretch of water, the vast majority of Scots have not responded
to the Troubles by taking sides and attitudes towards Northern
Ireland seem not that different from those prevalent in England. In
1992 35 per cent of Scots were in favour of Northern Ireland
remaining part of the United Kingdom – only six percentage points
ahead of the English. By 2001 sentiment in the two countries had
converged: only 26 per cent of Scots and 25 per cent of the English
were in favour of Ulster remaining British. A militant anti-Catholic
might want to present the recent history of Northern Ireland as proof
of the evils of Romanism; most Scots of all religions see it as proof of
the evils of mixing religion and politics.

The Old Firm

The Glasgow derby between Rangers and Celtic is over a century
old and remains the UK's biggest domestic football fixture. The two
clubs have dominated the Scottish game. Both command a huge fan
base, with supporters' buses travelling from every town in Scotland
and beyond. And both have considerable support in Northern
Ireland (though Manchester United remains the best supported club
in the province).[5] Of course, successful teams will always attract large
crowds and the best players, and fathers will always socialise their sons

into supporting the same team, but the pull of the Glasgow clubs goes beyond this. The Old Firm has two sets of supporters segregated by more than just the seating arrangements.

Rangers FC has a firm Protestant Unionist identity. Many of its official supporters' clubs incorporate the words 'Loyal' or 'True Blues' into their names. Supporters carry Union Jacks, the Red Hand of Ulster and scarves adorned with images of King William of Orange. Terrace songs include the Orange battle anthems of 'The Sash' and 'No Pope of Rome', while many more songs include anti-Catholic lyrics. Celtic FC, on the other hand, has an Irish Catholic identity. Its fans carry the Irish tricolour and sing Irish folk or rebel political ballads such as 'Fields of Athenry' and 'The Boys of the Old Brigade'.

Old Firm rivalry is often interpreted as a symptom of deep and enduring sectarianism. Certainly, several English-based television documentaries and news reports have portrayed the Old Firm as representatives of a religious divide, while the more sensational coverage has referred to 'warring tribes' in a city divided by 'sectarian hatred'.[6] It is, therefore, important to establish to what extent football and marching are symptomatic of a wider social cleavage. We will briefly explain how the Old Firm rivalry developed and consider its significance.

Glasgow Celtic was founded by the Marist Brother Walfrid in November 1887, as a charitable organisation to raise money to provide free dinners, clothing and other relief for the poor of the East End of Glasgow. Murray suggests deeper motives:

> Walfrid was also prompted by a fear that protestant soup-kitchens might tempt young catholics into apostasy. Moreover he was equally worried about the dangers of young catholics meeting protestants in their place of employment or leisure . . . A catholic football club, then, could serve the dual purpose of easing the pain in starving stomachs at the same time as it kept young catholics together in their leisure time, free from the temptations of protestants and protestantism.[7]

Rangers FC, which provided the opposition for Celtic's first game, had been formed sixteen years earlier. The relationship between the teams was friendly by all accounts. There were sound financial reasons for this: they were the two best-supported teams in Scotland

and cooperated to ensure maximum profit from gate receipts.[8] Conviviality between the club management did not extend out to the supporters. Fan violence, though not exactly commonplace, was not unknown.

Rangers had close links with the Clyde shipyards, which employed skilled Protestant workers, many from Ulster. As early as 1886, potential Rangers players were offered work via the foremen as an inducement to join the club, while the arrival of the Belfast-owned Harland & Wolff yard in 1912 helped sharpen Rangers' Protestant identity.[9] The club's no-Catholic signing policy is thought to have become institutionalised from the 1920 onwards, when Bill Struth became the Rangers' manager; his residency lasted until 1954. Sir John Ure Primrose, the chairman of Rangers, was a local Unionist politician and businessman who sat on the platform at Edward Carson's anti-home-rule rally in Glasgow in 1913.[10] Previously, he had split from the Liberal Party over the home-rule issue in 1887 and became identified with the club the following year.

Celtic has always been a Catholic team in the sense that its supporters, club officials and players have always been predominately Catholic. They have never been exclusively so; Jock Stein, their most successful manager, was Protestant, as were fans' favourites such as John Thompson, Kenny Dalglish and Danny McGrain. But that has not prevented the club or its fans maintaining its Irish Catholic ethos. The club came under attack from the Scottish Football Association in 1952, which ordered it to remove the Irish tricolour from the roof of Celtic Park, arguing that it had no connection with football or Scotland. Regarding this as an attack on its Irish roots, Celtic threatened to withdraw from the league and, when Rangers supported the club, the matter was dropped.[11] Celtic's Irish connection remains strong, with the tricolour still flying and the team continuing to play in green and white with the shamrock crest on the shirts.

When Celtic was being criticised for its Irish flag, Rangers escaped censure for its sectarian signing policy. That only came to public attention in the 1960s. The decisive change in Rangers came in the late 1980s when the former Liverpool star Graeme Souness was signed as player-manager. Souness persuaded his friend David Murray to buy a controlling interest in the club. Murray was an Edinburgh businessman with no connections with Orangeism or unionism and as an outsider he was well suited to underwrite Souness's ambitious plan to modernise the club. His first innovation was to sign English football stars. His second was to sign a Catholic.[12]

Mo Johnston, a Catholic from a mixed marriage, was a popular Celtic player who, after a spell in French football, agreed to return to the Parkhead club. Instead, largely through the actions of his agent Bill McMurdo (who was a founder of the Scottish Unionist Party), he became Rangers' first prominent Catholic player. Some Rangers fans burned their scarves and season tickets in front of the cameras, while graffiti messages such as 'Souness you Roman Bastard' appeared on some city walls. Celtic supporters viewed Johnston as a traitor of the worst kind. The paramilitary-style slogan 'Collaborators can't play without kneecaps' appeared outside Bellgrove railway station close to Celtic Park. The story made Scottish front page news for over a week and drew worldwide attention. But the crowds did not stay away. Rather the Ibrox ground was expanded to allow more fans to cheer on more Catholic players. In the late 1990s there were seven or eight Catholics in the squad, including Neil McCann, a Scot of Irish descent, and the Argentinian Gabriel Amato, who blessed himself before entering the field of play. The Italian Catholic Lorenzo Amoruso was followed as captain by Barry Ferguson, whose own identity and beliefs ably illustrate the gap between myth and reality. As he put it: 'I've been portrayed as this mad Rangers Orangeman total nut. It's daft. I grew up as a Rangers fan but I've got friends that grew up as Celtic fans.' His wife Margaret, whom he had dated since they were both 16, is a Catholic. His only child of school age goes to a Catholic school. His reply to the question of whether he believed in God is worth quoting at length because it could probably stand for the views of most young Scots: 'No. I'm not religious at all. My mum and dad never bothered about religion either way. Margaret does religion with the kids and at school and that's up to her. That doesn't bother me one little bit.'[13]

RITUAL ABUSE

Although the managements of both clubs have taken major steps to discourage their fans from displaying sectarian attitudes, a considerable portion of the support on both sides has refused to cooperate with this modernisation. Some Celtic fans continue to demonstrate their approval of the IRA; some Rangers fans chant their support for

the UVF. When 20,000 Scots of one religious and ethnic background regularly chant their hatred for all those of an alternative
background, we might suppose that Scotland is indeed endemically
sectarian. However, that such florid sectarianism occurs in the
context of supporting rival football teams should cause us to think
a little longer. There are good reasons for supposing that most of
those people do not mean it.

An important place to start is with social class. Many Old Firm fans
are urban working class. They have been raised in a culture in which
coarse language is normal, in which people routinely shout at each
other and in which casual violence is commonplace. This is an
important point. If a normally polite middle-class person were to
shout 'Fuck the Pope', we might reasonably take this as indicating a
deep hatred for the Pope. If someone who says 'fuckin'' three times in
most sentences shouts 'Fuck the Pope' it may signify a good deal less.

Much football fan behaviour is highly ritualised. Since the days of
the Roman coliseums, the stadium has provided a setting that
encourages spectators to participate vocally and take sides to reflect
the athletes' rivalry on the ground below. Rival football supporters,
who can represent different neighbourhoods, cities or countries,
deliberately exaggerate their differences by drawing on a variety of
material for purpose of ritual insult. In the mid-1980s supporters of
London teams regularly taunted the fans of rivals from the north of
England by singing about their dire employment prospects. Aberdeen fans borrowed the idea and sometimes still sing 'You'll never get
a job. Sign on! Sign on!' (to the tune of 'You'll Never Walk Alone')
to annoy Old Firm fans. Urban fans 'noise up' those from a rural area
about the sexual appeal of farmyard animals. And Old Firm supporters draw on historical events in Ireland to antagonise each other.
The important thing is the wind-up. When the IRA prisoner Bobby
Sands was dying on hunger strike, a number of Rangers' supporters
hung skeletons at the windows of their buses. This does not
necessarily mean they had strongly held views about the Ulster
conflict. It just means they wanted to annoy the fans of their greatest
rival.

A football match takes place in a particular place at a particular
time, and the aggressive posturing and offensive chanting that
accompany it are largely contained within the immediate margins
of that location and time. Of course, football is capable of breeding

'afters', aided by drink and on-field controversy, but football-related disorder has occurred in most cities, with much of it being far more extreme than Glasgow has ever experienced.[14]

It is worth adding an aside about the way in which context influences the priority that people give to their various possible identities. In the previous chapter we noted that both the Scottish Social Attitudes survey and the Glasgow survey failed to produce evidence that Scottish Catholics (even those who were Celtic supporters) thought of themselves as Irish. This is in stark contrast to Joseph Bradley's claims based on a small survey of football fans.[15] The explanation may be that, because Bradley contacted respondents at football matches and gave a lot of attention to football in his questions, respondents were subtly encouraged to dwell on sentiments associated with football. The two large surveys were administered by professional interviewers in the homes of respondents. Away from the match and the thoughts of the game, sectarian identities might seem a lot less significant.

A final point worth noting is that the current structure of Scottish football has given Old Firm fans an unusual reason to posture in attitudes of ritual hatred: the absence of other rivals. In most leagues five or six clubs regularly compete for the top honours. Celtic and Rangers have only each other as serious rivals. Some of the intensity of that competition derives from the zero-sum nature of their contest. A Celtic loss increases the chances of Rangers winning a title and vice versa to an extent that is not found in the competition between, say, Arsenal and Fulham in the English Premiership.

We stress the context because, if it is ignored, the intensity of Old Firm rivalry can easily be taken to reflect the seriousness of the rivalry between the religious and ethnic identities that are, for some fans, represented by Rangers and Celtic.[16] Football rivalry is a social force in its own right that should not, without considerable scaling down, be taken to stand for anything else. Or at least, before we make much of the Old Firm, we should remember that, after the match, very many of those fans will, like the captain of the treble-winning 2002 Rangers team, go home to one of the very people, whom for ninety minutes they ritually abuse.

Sectarian Violence: Creating a Moral Panic

'Stop Glasgow's Killing Fields' screamed a *Scotland on Sunday* headline in 2001. In the accompanying article, Cara Henderson, the founder of campaigning organisation Nil by Mouth, described her first Old Firm game. In an interesting display of the ability to sustain a preconception in the face of refuting evidence, she asserted that there was violence after every Old Firm game and then ruefully added: 'nobody was murdered within hours of the final whistle, a state of affairs provoking surprise among the Glasgow constabulary, which has grown wearily accustomed to weeding out killers from both communities – but especially the Protestant sector.'[17] 'Weeding out killers' is strong stuff. In an article written for an academic journal in 2003, James Conroy bolstered his assertion that Scotland remained a place of discrimination and bigotry by claiming that eleven Rangers and Celtic fans had been murdered since 1995: more than one a year.[18] In a 2002 news release announcing a Church and Nation Committee report on sectarianism, the Church of Scotland's press office said that committee members had heard 'a chilling catalogue of repeated violence sparked by a mixture of football and sectarian division'.[19] In 2003 the web site of the Scottish Council for Voluntary Organisations (SCVO) said: 'There have been more sectarian murders than race-related murders in Scotland over the past decade.'[20]

What is clear from the Glasgow City survey is that when most people say that sectarianism is a major problem they have in mind football-related violence.[21] When we have discussed sectarianism at meetings and with friends, it is Scotland's high rate of sectarian murder that is most often presented as evidence.

When we looked at the Catholic record in the labour market, we made the point that widely held perceptions can be wrong. Here we make the same assertion: widely held beliefs about the incidence of sectarian violence are simply wrong. In the case of people believing that certain occupations are closed to them because of their religion, we suspect the origins are historical. Judgements based on some experiences in the past live on and are amplified in the collective memory. The past doubtless plays a part in myths about sectarian violence: the stories of the Bridgeton Billy Boys and their Catholic counterparts are frequently repeated. But the myth of sectarian violence is perpetuated by people who have an interest in scaring us, and the rest of this chapter shows how a kernel of truth becomes falsehood by arithmetical error, exaggeration and repetition.

What is remarkable about the assertions of the importance of sectarian violence with which we began this section is that Conroy, the Kirk, SCVO, Nil by Mouth, and the various newspapers that have repeated these claims were all using the same one source. We will now show how this dubious consensus was created.

The *Sunday Herald* uncritically reported Peter Maclean, a spokesman for Nil by Mouth, saying: 'Eight murders with a sectarian element in the last few years – mostly in and around the Glasgow area – is an issue that shouldn't be minimised.'[22] A few months earlier he had told the Justice 2 Committee of the Scottish Parliament: 'in 1999–2000 no racially motivated murders were recorded. However, Nil by Mouth has researched sectarian-related offences and has found eight murders during that time that had a clear sectarian element.' This was no slip of the tongue. Six months earlier he had given the same figure to the *Daily Record*: 'Our statistics for 1999–2000 show no racist murders but at least eight sectarian murders in Scotland.'[23] The same claim was repeated in a newsletter in 2003.

In its 2002 report on sectarianism, the Church of Scotland's Church and Nation Committee claimed the deaths of 'eleven Rangers and Celtic football fans since 1995'.[24] When we asked for the source of this figure, we were referred to a report written by Dr Elinor Kelly, of the University of Glasgow, and Gregory Graham. This same source was the one used by Nil by Mouth.

Kelly and Graham identify eleven Old Firm-related murders between 1984 and 2001: a span of eighteen years. In that period there were 2,099 homicides at an average of 116 a year.[25] Hence, according to Kelly and Graham, the proportion of Scottish homicides that are sectarian was 0.5 per cent. But when the Church of Scotland used the same research, someone mistakenly reduced the period over which the eleven murders has occurred to just seven years: more than doubling the apparent rate of sectarian killing. Finally, Nil by Mouth, reading the same research, reduced the number of murders to eight but shortened the timescale even further to just two years so that 3.4 per cent of murders were now sectarian. It is important that we appreciate the extent of exaggeration here: Kelly and Graham identify eleven sectarian murders but Nil by Mouth end up repeatedly asserting a rate that would have created sixty-eight such homicides.

Now that we have identified the inflation of the Kelly and Graham figures, we can consider the accuracy of their designations. When Donald Gorrie MSP first proposed his bill to add an additional penalty to crimes that are committed for sectarian motives, many people (including police representatives) pointed out that it is often hard to know exactly why someone is killed. Nonetheless Kelly and Graham have made judgements about eleven murders and, if we are going to test their claims, we need to cover the same ground. A detailed examination will also be useful for suggesting alternative explanation.

THE CASES

We will describe the cases cited by Kelly and Graham and add further information gleaned from our reading of newspaper accounts and details given in court proceedings.

1. In April 1984, Alan Preston went to an Old Firm game with some Celtic fans. Fighting broke out at Partick station and Preston died after being dragged under a train. Three teenagers were charged with murder. As this death occurred during fighting between Old Firm fans, we agree it should be regarded as 'sectarian' in the Kelly and Graham sense.

2. In May 1989, according to Kelly and Graham, 'James McCluskie . . . died from stab wounds after a street battle between two neighbouring families that supported Celtic and Rangers as they watched the Cup Final on television'. According to the *Evening Times* report of the case:

> violence broke out the day fans watched the final on television in neighbouring houses. It ended with father-of-four McCluskie dying in the street from stab wounds. The court heard the trouble started when Celtic scored the winning goal. A woman ran shouting from McCluskie's house and an Irish tricolour was waved. There was an angry response from a house across the road where a Union Jack was brandished in retaliation. There was trouble in the street for hours outside McCluskie's home.

McCluskie's murder could reasonably be described as sectarian.

3. In October 1995 Mark Scott was attacked by Jason Campbell as he walked through Bridgeton following a Celtic–Partick Thistle game – the case described at the start of this chapter. This is sectarian.

4 and 5. In September 1997 Paul O'Neill and Robert McCann
died from stab wounds in a general affray. According to the *Herald*:

> Mr Vance [the police officer leading the investigation] also
> confirmed yesterday that sectarian songs were being sung on
> the streets near the scene of the fatal incident in the early hours of
> Sunday, just hours after an Old Firm reserve match at nearby
> Ibrox stadium . . . However, Mr Vance played down the sectarian
> connection, saying there was nothing to suggest it had led to the
> double murder. Mr Vance added: 'We have information that
> witnesses heard songs from both sides of the sectarian divide being
> sung, but I am sure that isn't an unusual occurrence on a Saturday
> evening. I have absolutely no evidence that these directly resulted
> in the violence which occurred, although at this stage we have not
> completely ruled that out . . . However, despite the latest in-
> formation, we have not yet got a firm motive for the incident. We
> have a number of options about the reasons for this outbreak of
> extreme violence but we have not converted that into hard
> evidence. At this stage we still do not know what the catalyst
> was.'[26]

The next day's *Herald* quoted DCI Vance saying: 'this bears the
hallmarks of a local dispute.' Jason Andrew Campbell (who remark-
ably, given the rarity of the Christian name, is not the Jason
Campbell of UVF fame) and Thomas Docherty were accused that,
while acting with others, they did form part of a disorderly crowd,
shout, swear and sing sectarian songs, assault Charles Galloway to his
injury, and murder Robert McCann by repeatedly striking him with
knives or similar instruments. On 6 January 1998 Campbell was
admonished and Docherty was jailed for six years.

As the charge of 'singing sectarian songs' was dropped from the
indictment during court proceedings and there is nothing else to
indicate a sectarian motive, we see no reason to code this murder as
sectarian.

6. In May 1999, according to Kelly and Graham: 'John
Ormiston . . . Rangers fan died after being beaten up in West
Lothian after an Old Firm game.' The details given in court suggest
something rather different. Ormiston had been involved in a serious
road accident that had left him with a damaged spleen. He drank
heavily and had a reputation for pestering women at his regular

haunt: the Fa'side Inn in Wallyford, East (not West) Lothian. Justin Smith, 23, was in the pub on 2 May 1999, when his girlfriend went to the bar to order drinks. Ormiston grabbed hold of her. She stuck her elbow into him and shouted to her boyfriend: 'Get rid of this idiot.' Smith and Ormiston went outside, where Smith punched Ormiston on the body, knocked him to the ground, then punched and kicked him again. The victim apparently offered no resistance. Afterwards, the two men shook hands and Ormiston went back to the bar for another drink before making his way home. The next morning he told his uncle he was not going to work. The uncle left under the impression that Ormiston had a hangover. Later that day he returned to find his nephew dead. Although the fight occurred the same day as an Old Firm game, nothing in the evidence suggested that football or religion had anything to do with the incident.

7. In May 1999, after the cup final, 'Thomas McFadden, a Celtic fan, was chased by Peter Rushford and stabbed by David Hutton.' The details given in court suggest this was sectarian.

8. In August 1999, according to Kelly and Graham: 'George Reid (40) Celtic fan, murdered by Patrick Nicol (17) after Nicol's Rangers shirt was accidentally burned in a pub'. In this terse description, the Rangers shirt is central but the full details paint a very different picture.

According to the court reports, Reid was an alcoholic of no fixed abode who spent his time begging and drinking.[27] He often slept in a friend's flat in the block where Nicol lived. On 6 August 1999 Nicol used part of his holiday pay to buy a new Rangers football top, which he wore that evening. He drank a large amount of alcohol during the afternoon and evening and in the later part of the evening he spent some time in the Falcon Bar, Stirling, where his new top was accidentally burned by a fellow customer. This upset Nicol, who became aggressive. Some time after 2 o'clock the following morning Nicol met Reid. According to Nicol's recollection – not disputed by the Crown in the appeal – there was some physical contact between the deceased and Nicol, which Nicol construed as an unwelcome sexual overture. His reaction was both instantaneous and uncontrolled. He repeatedly stabbed Reid with a large kitchen knife.

What is clear from the court details but missing from the Kelly and

Graham version is that the man Nicol attacked was not the person who had burnt his shirt. That had happened earlier in the day. The trigger for the attack was an unwanted sexual advance. There is no reason to code this as sectarian.

9. In August 2000, James Hardie, a Rangers fan, was killed by Celtic fan Gary Rodgers on his doorstep in Drumchapel after an Old Firm game. Although they count this case as sectarian, Kelly and Graham say: 'The trial did not confirm suspicions that the murder was sectarian motivated.' The court evidence showed that Rodgers slashed Hardie because he was told that Hardie had made insulting remarks about his mother. We support Kelly and Graham's original judgement: this was not obviously sectarian.

10. The same month, Brian Sweeney, a Celtic fan, was stabbed and killed by William Wingate, who also attacked Sweeney's brother. This street fight was not related to any Old Firm match; the nearest took place a fortnight later. The only discernible link to the Old Firm is that the victim was a Celtic fan. It would appear that Kelly and Graham regard this as football related because football fans created a shrine of scarves that was destroyed by vandals. But this tells us about *responses* to a Celtic shrine. It says nothing about the causes of Sweeney's death. There is no evidence that football or religion played any part in Wingate's attack on the Sweeney brothers and no reason to judge this as sectarian.

11. On 4 December 2000 Mark Fox stabbed and killed Frank Forrester Jr in Fenwick. The background was a long-running dispute between Fox and the Forrester family that had allegedly involved, among many other things, the victim's father taunting Fox over Rangers' 5–1 victory in an Old Firm game two weeks earlier. Fox had eight previous convictions (including a firearms charge); the affray that led to the death did not involve the person who had allegedly insulted Fox's team; and there was a history of family rivalry. This suggests that the attack was not entirely or even primarily a sectarian murder. Nonetheless, so that we cannot be accused of stacking the odds in our favour, we will record this as a sectarian killing.

Those are the eleven murder cases claimed as sectarian by Kelly and Graham. Since they wrote their report we have found two more:

12. According to the *Daily Record*:

A teenager in a Celtic strip battered a boozy Rangers fan to death after an Old Firm match, a court heard yesterday. Steven Jardine, 39, had watched Celtic beat his team on TV in the pub where his wife worked as a barmaid until she ordered him home.

Two girls told the High Court in Glasgow they saw 19-year-old postman Stephen McMillan knock Mr Jardine down in Govan, Glasgow, and kick and stamp on him. Mr Jardine never regained consciousness and died in hospital from head injuries nearly two months later.

Advocate depute Brian Connachie said: 'The girls described the victim's head bouncing off the ground as he was kicked and stamped on.' McMillan, of Orkney Street, Govan, who was originally charged with murder, admitted a reduced charge of culpable homicide. Sentence was deferred until next month for reports, and McMillan was released on bail.[28]

13. We add this case because it formally has all the ingredients that Kelly and Graham use to select murders. According to the *Daily Record*:

A Celtic fan was yesterday convicted of murdering a fellow supporter as they celebrated a 3–0 victory over Rangers. Thug Stephen Nisbet, 28, shouted: 'Out the window with him' before David James, 37, was thrown from the first floor of a flat. Nisbet and two other men, Dominic Ferrie, 24, and Stewart Quinn, 30, then stamped on his head and battered his body with broken concrete slabs. Ferrie and Quinn were jailed for life in February for the murder, on April 30, 2001. Quinn is serving a minimum 18-year sentence and Ferrie is serving a minimum 14 years. Nisbet now faces a life sentence.

At the High Court in Glasgow yesterday, cheering women were ejected from the public benches when the majority verdict was delivered. The court heard the Celtic fans celebrated their victory at the Era Bar in Craigneuk, Lanarkshire, before going to the flat in Glencleland Road. Witness Gerard Hoey, 29, told the court he saw Nisbet, Quinn and Ferrie standing over James, who was face down on the floor with blood on his neck. He said he heard Nisbet shouting: 'Out of the window with him.' James was then dragged back into the bedroom.

No motive for the murder emerged during the trial. Nisbet was convicted of acting with Quinn and Ferrie and murdering Mr James, of Craigneuk. He was also found guilty of failing to appear for trial with them earlier this year. Charges of setting fire to the house where the attack took place and threatening a witness with violence were dropped.[29]

The important point about that case is that, while it is very similar to most of the others (in that it involves drunk young football fans), the victim supported the same club as the killers.

From our reading of the press reports and court details we conclude that, of the eleven homicides claimed by Kelly and Graham and the subsequent ones we have added, only six are arguably sectarian. In most of the others such football links as can be found (Nicol's Rangers top, for example) are simply background noise – there because most fatal attacks involve young working-class men, a high proportion of whom are football fans. To put the data in their proper context, only 0.3 per cent (that is, less than one-third of 1 per cent) of Scotland's homicides in the eighteen years being surveyed have been sectarian.

INTERPRETING THE DATA

The most obvious point about sectarian violence is that 99.5 per cent of Scottish homicides over the last twenty years were entirely innocent of it. That context is important. Imagining away the Reformation and football would make no appreciable difference to the levels of fatal violence in Scotland.

Second, we must remember what this argument is about. It would be possible to explain the above cases by noting that a number of young working-class men drink too much, take drugs, carry weapons and readily resort to physical violence. In 2003 a senior Cumbria policeman, reflecting on an apparent increase in casual violence, said:

> there seems to be a lot of general intolerance for anyone who is not local that can even extend to someone who is from a different town or village. There have been occasions of someone going from Carlisle to Penrith for a night out and getting attacked simply because they were from Carlisle, and vice-versa.[30]

Here the grounds for violence is foreignness in the weakest sense. As we see from the history of gang violence, groups that generate a sense of justification for attacking outsiders can be constructed without even residential area as a basis. People simply chose to join one gang or another. We could reasonably interpret the very small amount of sectarian violence we find as simply one, not very common, expression of a more general lack of civilisation.

But Kelly, Gorrie, the Kirk, Nil by Mouth and Conroy prefer to cite the above data as proof that Scotland is sectarian. Kelly was quite specific in her submission to the Church of Scotland that sectarianism was an independent and important cause of violence. Testing that claim is not easy, but our surveys do throw some light on the issue. In its section on crime, the Glasgow survey asked respondents if they had been physically attacked in the previous five years and, if so, for what reason. As we noted in the previous chapter, religion was not a significant factor. Nor was football. Out of 1,000 respondents, 147 said they had been attacked but only fourteen of these people gave 'football team' as the main reason for the attack.

The Scottish Crime Survey follows a similar method of asking a random sample of Scots what crimes they have suffered. In 1999 only 26 per cent of all crimes of violence were committed by strangers and in 88 per cent of those the assailant was under the influence of drinks or drugs.[31] If we look again at the cases detailed above, we see they conform almost perfectly to the model implied by these data. All involve working-class male brutality. In all cases the assailants (and in most cases the victims also) were drunk and were armed and responded to minor insults with a vicious attack. By and large murders fall into two sorts. Some two-thirds are committed by family members, intimate partners and acquaintances. A very large proportion of the rest occur as part of more general fights and affrays in which murder is not deliberate but is an accepted possible consequence. Of the homicides that occurred between 1984 and 2001 (the period of Kelly and Graham's study), three-quarters of the victims were male and in over half of the solved cases, the main accused was a male aged between 16 and 29. Around half of the male victims died from knife attacks and 60 per cent of the main accused were males aged 16 to 29. This group also produced almost half of the victims of fatal stabbings.

Street violence is the preserve of working-class men. Many

working-class men are football supporters. In the western Lowlands many football fans are Old Firm supporters. Hence many of the perpetrators and victims of street violence will be Old Firms fans simply by coincidence. Patrick Nicol (case 8 above) already had a conviction for assault and robbery before the events that Kelly and Graham classify as sectarian violence. This may seem flippant but we can make the point by saying that a lot of young working-class men who engage in casual violence have tattoos. But it is obvious that the tattoo itself is not a cause of the murder. We would not describe them as tattoo murders. Imagine that the Old Firm vanished (as did all memory of them) and their places were taken by two teams – Glasgow East and Glasgow South – that had no ethnic or religious ties but that were extremely popular and regularly competing for the same prizes. Do we think that the level of violence would be markedly lower?

One reason for thinking not is that, contrary to assertions made in evidence to the Church of Scotland's Church and Nation Committee, Old Firm games are not unusual among local derby matches in generating violence. After the Manchester derby of November 2000, large groups of City fans, some carrying smoke bombs and distress flares, attacked United supporters. There were several outbreaks of fighting and dozens of arrests were made. The following month police arrested more than thirty people when hundreds of rival Sheffield fans clashed after the first United–Wednesday game in seven years. Officers wearing riot gear used CG gas and batons to pacify the mobs. At the March 2003 Old Firm game, nineteen people were arrested; the week before forty-two fans were arrested during a Birmingham City–Aston Villa derby and three policemen were hospitalised. But we need not rely on anecdotes, which can be selectively recalled: we have arrest data for twelve Old Firm games between August 2000 and December 2002. There was an average of just 12.3 arrests per game.[32]

Although it relates to 1976, it is worth citing some details of a report produced by the Statistics Branch of Strathclyde police for the Association of Chief Police Officers.[33] It examined 270 senior football games in Scotland. The vast majority of offences, were breaches of the peace and assaults. Together there were 1,079 offences, which it calculated represented 7.32 offences per 100,000 spectators per hour. With wonderful dryness, the author says: 'it seems probable that this compares very favourably with the number of arrests made for Breach of the Peace and Assault each hour per 100,000 persons engaged in their various forms of leisure activity on a Saturday night.' The report compares Rangers and Celtic fans with those of other clubs and concludes that they 'have only an average or lower than average number of arrests per 1,000 spectators at their home games'. The McElhone report also examined the bigger question of the effects of football matches on crime reports and arrest figures for towns hosting games by comparing data for days when games were played with comparable days when there was no game. It concluded that there was no significant difference. In some cases crime rates actually fell on match days. The overall conclusion was that there was no more crime, disorder and violence associated with football than was present normally. Football fans did what they, and others, normally do on Saturdays and among that repertoire of activities there would be some crime and disorder.

THE CAUSES OF BAD BEHAVIOUR

Scotland has its fair share of anti-social behaviour. The papers regularly report breaches of the peace, fights and attempted arson attempts. And a very small proportion of them have some sort of sectarian element to them. For example, in 2003 members of an Ardrossan family were convicted of breaches of the peace for shouting sectarian abuse at their neighbours, one of whom was a Catholic.[34] Mr Smith, as we shall call him, his wife, and her two adult children had taunted their downstairs neighbours a number of times. On the evening in question they came home drunk, sang sectarian songs and banged on the floor. When the police arrived, Smith told them: 'See that young boy downstairs. I'm going to kick the shit out of him.'

If we are going to maintain that this sort of things proves that Scotland is a sectarian society, we must believe that had the Smiths and their neighbours been of the same religion, there would not have been trouble between them. We do not believe that. From their previous records and general demeanour it seems pretty likely that the Smiths would have found other ostensible reasons to quarrel with people. The religious division is not the primary reason for the dispute. It merely provides one party with a convenient language of abuse when one is needed. We are minded of the case of two young boys in London who harassed an elderly Jewish couple by painting a swastika on their front door. When the police questioned the boys, it became clear that they had no idea what the swastika represented. Nor did they dislike Jews in particular. They were just anti-social scumbags who liked upsetting people and they had been told by older boys that a swastika would put the wind up these people.

He might be wrong, but William Rae, the chief constable of Strathclyde, is presumably as well placed as anyone to appreciate the importance of sectarian violence on his patch. In his June 2003 report he described the levels of violent crime as 'nothing short of disgraceful' and specifically cited binge drinking and the carrying of weapons. He did not mention sectarianism.[35]

To return to where we started, we have something of a paradox. In so far as we can measure these things, the Old Firm does not generate a disproportionate amount of violence. Nor apparently, does religio-ethnic identity. Yet many people think there is a major problem and there is widespread support for legislative action. As the Glasgow City Council study neatly summarised it: 'Two-thirds of respondents perceived sectarian violence to be very or quite common in Glasgow. However, less than one percent of all respondents said that in the last five years, their religion had been the cause of a physical attack against them.'[36] Only a similar number think that their football team was the reason for being attacked.

Which takes us into our next question.

WHY DO PEOPLE GET IT WRONG?

Most people are not in a position to check what they see and hear in the media. When they read a lot about sectarian violence, they do not stop to ask if it is really likely that there are five Old Firm-related murders every year. What is more disturbing is that a journalist, an academic with no background in empirical research, a Church of Scotland committee with no social-science researchers on it and a publicly funded campaigning organisation have all contributed to the creation of a moral panic.

There is no mystery about why journalists exaggerate: it sells copies. Newsprintworld is a dreadful place of fear and loathing. For example, in 1998 *Scotland on Sunday* ran a story under the headline 'Celtic fans seek new rail station to bypass gauntlet of knife attacks'.[37] 'Gauntlet of knife attacks' means a row of people, armed with knives, attacking everyone who has to pass them. Only if you read into the body of the story did you find the fact that Strathclyde police said that only two assaults had been reported to it in two years. Sometimes the journalist's desire to produce a sense of crisis is only too apparent. In July 2000 BBC Scotland reported a trivial story about a Glasgow University trust fund, set up by a nineteenth-century evangelical Protestant, to help fund the education of indigent Christians. That Glasgow University continued to administer a trust, the proceeds of which were available only to evangelicals, was regarded as a disgrace. The story said: 'The Catholic chaplain . . . would not be drawn on whether the trust could heighten sectarian sentiment in Glasgow.'[38] That 'would not be drawn' rather gives the game away. You can just hear the keen young journalist egging the chaplain on to say 'This will cause blood to run in the streets'. Another example of a sectarian gloss being given to a story concerns the sad death of a brave young man. When Thomas Loughrey passed a young man hitting his girlfriend in a Glasgow street, he intervened and was stabbed to death for his troubles. Football and ethnicity had nothing at all to do with the killing, but when the *Herald* reported the verdict of the trial it did so under the headline: 'Fifteen years for killing Celtic fan'.[39] To cite another example: in November 1988 a young man stabbed and killed another when he tried to extort money from a group of acquaintances. The only Old Firm association is that the assailant had spent the afternoon watching a Ranger– Celtic game on TV. There was no suggestion at all that the victims of the intended extortion were chosen on the basis of football allegiance, religion or ethnicity; they just happened to be handy when the thug decided he needed some money. Yet the *Herald* ran the story of the court verdict under the headline 'Attack after Old Firm match'.[40] Sectarianism is a convenient frame in which to dramatise stories and through which to present aspects of Scotland. It is a cliché deployed even in stories that are apparently intended to document the reality. For example, an article on Orange walks in the supposedly serious *New Society* in the 1980s said '12 July now rarely ends in mass bloodshed'[41] but continued to suggest the annual parades were of great social significance because they still contained the potential for serious violence. The magazine's editor did not have the wit to ask the journalist to specify just when a Scottish Orange walk had last ended in 'mass bloodshed'.

We might also add that newspaper staffing levels are now about half of what they were before the 1980s revolution in print technology. Many journalists are young, inexperienced and lacking in the time or the research skills to investigate stories in detail or properly to understand their contexts. Hence the tendency to stereotyping and to uncritical repetition.

There is no mystery about why Nil by Mouth gets it wrong. It is a campaigning organisation that will exist only so long as it persuades funders that there is a huge problem that it can help solve; its staff have a career interest in finding sectarian violence.[42] Donald Gorrie MSP is a politician who wishes to rid the world of sectarianism. In order to mobilise political support he must persuade us all that the problem is very very big. And, the bigger the sectarian dragon, the greater the kudos for slaying it. The Kirk's error seems to have been produced by a combination of guilt and poor arithmetic. The Kirk has changed so much since the 1930s that it is ashamed of its previous positions. To justify its apology for its earlier racism it feels it must show that sectarianism is very very bad. When its researcher makes a mistake, the Church and Nation Committee does not notice because the grossly exaggerated figure fits expectations. It may be that no one in the General Assembly thought the sectarian murder rate figure implausible. Or it may be that some suspected exaggeration but were unwilling to argue about it for fear of being taken to be anti-Catholic.

At every stage in the creation of this myth there was little willingness to check. The convenor of the Justice 2 Committee did press Peter McLean on the evidence for his claim,[43] but his failure to give an answer was not reported. When we raised the error with the Church of Scotland, the Deputy Clerk referred us to the researcher who helped prepare the committee report. When we contacted the researcher, she simply said: 'this information came from Dr Elinor Kelly'[44] and ignored our point that the Kirk had mistakenly doubled the rate that Kelly and Graham claimed. When we sent an early draft of our conclusions to Donald Gorrie and drew his attention both to the possibility of very different interpretations of the original cases and to the fact that Nil by Mouth's numbers could not be reconciled with Kelly's, Gorrie ignored the points of substance and wrote: ' To pretend it [i.e. sectarian murder] doesn't exist is as disturbing as any possible exaggeration by Nil by Mouth.'[45]

Thus far our explanation of the myth has two parts: the real experience of a small and geographically confined problem and the material interests of those responsible for creating the myth. But we would like to add a third part. We do not want to make too much of this but we suspect that the myth is popular because it fits with a fairly widespread desire of Scots to imagine their country as a gritty, seamy, violent place.

It is difficult to make this point except by anecdote, but it is worth considering the sorts of cultural products that are currently popular in Scotland. Since it first appeared in 1983, the series *Taggart*, featuring a hard-bitten Glasgow cop and a large cast of corpses, has been STV's most successful programme. Greenock-born Peter McDougall has been one of Scotland's most successful playwrights. Such works as *Just a Boy's Game* (starring the gritty-voiced rock singer Frankie Miller) and *Down among the Big Boys* (starring Billy Connolly) have at their heart working-class violence and crime. Jimmy Boyle, convicted killer-turned-sculptor and author, was a prominent figure in Scotland's arts world in the 1980s and 1990s. Two of Scotland's most successful contemporary painters – Ken Currie and Peter Howson – specialise in depicting working-class heroes and scenes of violence. Until his drying-out and return to the Catholic faith of his childhood, Howson was a hard-drinking, often violent, body-building drug-abuser.[46] We might add the novels of William McIlvanney, Ian Rankin, Christopher Brookmyre or James Kelman. Ron Mackay's *Mean City* was a deliberate homage to Alexander McArthur and Kingsley Long's *No Mean City*, a crime thriller based on the life of John Ross, the man who succeeded Billy Fullerton as leader of the Bridgeton Billy Boys. In bringing the McArthur and Long fiction up to date, Mackay seems to have modelled the characters and events closely on the life of the real-life gangster Arthur Thompson and his family. Even Scots comedy fuels the stereotypes. Scotland's most popular comedian, Billy Connolly, swears frequently during an act that used to feature episodes from his life as a working-class Glaswegian: shipyards and all. The much-loved character Rab. C. Nesbitt is an alcoholic down and out from Govan's 'Wine Alley' who happily describes himself as a 'scumbag'.

The idea that Glaswegians are particularly violent is so well established in British popular culture that it provides a convenient artistic shorthand. If a drama based in England wishes to introduce a tough cop or a sadistic villain, the author just gives the character a Glaswegian accent. It is interesting to note that, even when this stereotype is taken up by Scots themselves and altered, the kernel of the 'tough nut' remains in place. For example, Scottish football fans have since the 1980s presented themselves as the friendly fans, but that presentation is based not on weakness but on the proposition that 'We could chin the bastards if we wanted to but we don't need to prove anything'. It is not a rejection of machismo but a claim to a higher machismo. Like the stance of the Samurai, the Scottish fan now claims to be so hard that displays of hardness are unnecessary.[47]

The Glasgow of street gangs and organised crime is an extremely popular cultural production. The *Herald* in 2002 ran a special 'Herald Reader Offer' for a book entitled *Glasgow's Hard Men* with the enticing text:

> For more than 100 years Glasgow was known worldwide for its gangsters, villains and violence. From the slums and the deprived areas of the city came the hard men, the gangs and the godfathers . . . packed full of images from the archives of Scotland's leading newspapers . . . to receive your copy by Christmas please ensure that your order . . .

Of course, crime is a universally popular subject for novels, films and television programmes, but we think it plausible to suggest that many Scots are particularly attracted to the idea that Scotland is a land of hard men because it provides a way of asserting superiority over the English. The transformation of the 'Tartan Army' shows this. Scots football fans started to present themselves as being above violence at the same time as skinhead English fans were earning an international reputation for hooliganism: the Scots transformation was deliberately intended to form a clear contrast with the English.

The veteran journalist Murray Ritchie concluded a column in which he criticised Scots writers for an obsession with 'the downside' by saying:

> Anyone from outside Scotland seeing a McDougall play or reading any of the above works would get an impression of life in our country just as untypical as anything represented by the kailyard [nineteenth-century romanticisation of small town life]. Not for a minute do I deny the usefulness or legitimacy of a

literary representation of life in Scotland which is deprived and forsaken; but there is more to our society than just that, so why glory in it?[48]

We suspect that part of the answer is 'because we are ambivalent about our comfortable owner-occupier middle-class lives'. There is a general tendency to suspect that progress has been bought at the price of losing our souls. Though neither would have wished them to have succeeded, Walter Scott and Robert Louis Stevenson romanticised the Jacobites (but only once they had been defeated). Though very few of us would wish to work down the mines or in the shipyards, a society of suburban home-owning office workers (and especially its male members) has a faint romantic suspicion that something vital and authentic has been lost in that economic advance and derives a vicarious thrill from the dark side of a world that, for them, has gone.[49]

In summary, our reading of the evidence does not support the claim that sectarian violence is commonplace. In common with most urban societies, Scotland has a thug problem; it does not particularly have a sectarian thug problem. Detailed examination of recent assertions about sectarian murder shows that a moral panic has been created from a combination of self-interested credulity, poor arithmetic and a general willingness on the part of the Scots public to sustain a stereotype that romanticises the lost world of the male manual worker and provides a convenient contrast with images of the English.

Conclusion

In this chapter we have looked closely at claims for the importance of sectarianism in three areas: responses to the Northern Ireland conflict, Old Firm football rivalry, and football-related street violence. Our conclusion is that none provides evidence for the assertion that Scotland is particularly sectarian. There has been very little spillover from Northern Ireland. No Scots politician has drawn any advantage from backing either nationalists or unionists and very few have tried. The Scottish churches have reacted to the war in Ulster by becoming more, not less ecumenical. For the general public the Troubles have been read not as showing the evils of Romanism or Protestantism but as showing what happens when people take religion too seriously.

The one area in which historic Irish–Catholic and Scots–Protestant–Unionist identities retain any salience is among some (and we stress some) of the fans of Celtic and Rangers. And here we have tried to make two important points that are often neglected. First, football fan behaviour is by-and-large ritualised and confined. The vast majority of those who sing their approval of the IRA and the UVF do nothing at all outside football matches to turn those words into reality. After the games they go home to their mixed residential areas and to their spouses (who are very likely to be of the other religio-ethnic identity or none) and the next day they go to work in their mixed workplaces where their football allegiances are reduced to a few words of light-hearted banter. Finally, we have questioned the accuracy of the data that lie behind a moral panic over sectarian murder.

Notes

1. *Sunday Express*,11 March 1973.
2. *Daily Record*, 19 February 1979.
3. *Glasgow Herald*, 17 June 1979.
4. In 2002 and 2003 Bruce was regularly contacted by usually very young and credulous journalists who wanted confirmation that Ulster terrorists were making great inroads into the Scots drugs trade. For example, the *Daily Record* (26 July 2002) claimed that Billy Moore, one of the notorious UVF Shankill Butchers murder gang, was regularly visiting Glasgow to coordinate drugs links.
5. In 2004 both Celtic and Rangers command gates of 50,000 or more and have attracted well over 100,000 on occasions in the past. An idea of their relative popularity can be got from the fact that the 1991 population figure for the old Motherwell District, which borders on Glasgow, was over 140,000, but Motherwell FC recorded an average gate of only 7,306 in season 1997/8. We are grateful to the club for supplying that figure.
6. The BBC2 documentary *Clash of the Titans*, screened in June 1999, is an example. The Old Firm was also examined in Channel 4's Cutting Edge programme *Gazza's Coming Home* (1996), and the same channel's Witness programme entitled *Faith, Flutes and Football* (1995). The Mo Johnston signing of 1989 gave rise to lengthy news bulletins focusing on the clubs, as did the Hampden riot of 1980.
7. B. Murray, *The Old Firm* (Edinburgh: Mainstream, 1984), p. 60.
8. Ibid. pp. 27–9.
9. Ibid. pp. 84–6.

10. G. Walker, 'There's not a team like the Glasgow Rangers: football and religious identity in Scotland', in G. Walker and T. Gallagher (eds), *Sermons and Battle Hymns: Protestant Popular Culture in Modern Scotland* (Edinburgh: Edinburgh University Press, 1990) p. 142.

11. G. P. T. Finn, 'Racism, religion and social prejudice: Irish Catholic clubs, soccer and Scottish society – II: Social identities and conspiracy theories', *History of Sport*, 8 (1991), pp. 390–1.

12. See Walker, 'There's not a team . . .' for a more detailed account of the club during this period.

13. *Herald Magazine*, 13 December 2003.

14. For example, the Old Firm contest in May 1999 was marred by pitch invasions, the referee was hit by a coin and over 100 arrests were made after the match. On the same weekend, riot police had to use live ammunition and water cannon to repel some 2,000 Feyenoord supporters rampaging through Rotterdam city centre following their team winning the Dutch league. Derby matches in Rome, Athens and Istanbul are noted for widespread violence, while both players and referees in South America have been murdered following incidents during matches.

15. J. M. Bradley, *Ethnic and Religious Identity in Modern Scotland: Culture, Politics and Football* (Aldershot: Avebury, 1995).

16. It is worth noting that the two social scientists most prominent in claiming that sectarianism is a vital social force in modern Scotland – Bradley and Finn – are students of sport, and of football in particular. Those social scientists who doubt such claims – ourselves, Paterson, McCrone, Curtice – are sociologists of religion and of politics.

17. *Scotland on Sunday*, 4 February 2001, p. 6.

18. J. Conroy, ' "Yet I live here": a reply to Bruce on Catholic education in Scotland', *Oxford Review of Education*, 29 (2003), p. 410.

19. 'Tackling the "Demon" of sectarianism in Scotland', www.churchofscotland.org.uk/gasectarianism. Downloaded 7 March 2003.

20. www.scvo.org.uk/equalities/priorities/religdiscrim.htm. Downloaded 14 February 2003.

21. NFO Social Research, *Sectarianism in Glasgow – Final Report* (2003), p.56.

22. *Sunday Herald*, 2 March 2003. The quote was used by Neil Mackay in a report on the Glasgow City Council sectarianism survey in which he incorporated some highly critical comments from Dr Kelly about the quality of the research. He did not solicit judgements from other academics. As people who seriously considered tendering for the research project but did not pursue it because we thought it too difficult to do well within budget, we believe the NFO Social Research work to be highly competent.

23. *Daily Record*, 7 May 2002.

24. Church and Nation Committee report to the General Assembly 2002: para. 1.2.

25. We are grateful to the Justice Statistics branch of the Scottish Executive for supplying these details.

26. *Herald*, 3 September 1997.

27. High Court of Justiciary Appeal, 11 April 2000.
28. *Daily Record*, 28 May 2003.
29. *Daily Record*, 5 June 2003.
30. *Cumberland News*, 28 November 2003.
31. 'Violence in Scotland: findings from the 2000 Scottish Crime Survey', www.scotland.gov.uk/cru/kd01/green/csvs-04.asp
32. We are grateful to Strathclyde police for supplying these data.
33. The statistical report is appended to the McElhone report, *Football Crowd Behaviour: Report by a Working Group Appointed by the Secretary of State for Scotland* (London: HMSO, 1977).
34. *Daily Record*, 30 April 2003.
35. *Herald*, 28 June 2003.
36. NFO Social Research, *Sectarianism in Glasgow – Final Report* (2003), p. 59.
37. *Scotland on Sunday*, 15 February 1998.
38. BBC Scotland web site, 27 January 2000.
39. 20 December 2003.
40. *Herald*, 15 September 1999.
41. *New Society*, 5 July 1985.
42. In 2002 Nil by Mouth was given £500,000 of National Lottery funding. It was also given £75,000 over three years by the Scottish Executive.
43. Justice 2 Committee, 3 December 2002: www.scottish.parliament.uk/official_report/cttee/just2–02/j202–4602.htm#Col2354 The Convenor of the committee later said: 'Although I accept the genuine nature of the evidence from Nil by Mouth, the organisation's research did not stand up to any real cross-examination' (www.scottish.parliament.uk/official_report/cttee/just2–02/j202–4902.htm#Col2438).
44. Maggie Lunan, e-mail, 20 February 2003.
45. Donald Gorrie, e-mail, 14 March 2003.
46. *Sunday Herald Magazine*, 6 April 2003.
47. We are grateful to our University of Aberdeen colleague Richard Giulianotti, who has extensively researched Scottish football fans, for this observation.
48. *Herald*, 5 September 1993.
49. We found one small example of the romanticising of manual labour in a news story about Motherwell MP Frank Roy's role in persuading the Irish Prime Minister that it was too dangerous for him to attend an Old Firm game in Glasgow. The *Herald* headlined a profile of Roy 'A man of steel accustomed to toughing it out' (9 February 2001). One of his colleagues, who should remain nameless, said ' "Numpty making arse of himself" would have been nearer the mark'. We should add that we have cited many examples from the *Herald* not because it is any more guilty of using easy stereotypes than other Scots papers; it is simply the paper we most often read and hence cuttings from it figure disproportionately in our files.

5 Why Bigotry Failed

Introduction

According to James MacMillan, 'The west of Scotland is still basically a carbon copy of the north of Ireland, without the bombs.'[1] In the previous chapters we have presented a very large body of evidence that, we believe, comprehensively refutes that assertion. In this final chapter we draw together the threads that have run through earlier parts of the book to explain why Glasgow is not Belfast and why the Irish Catholic experience in Scotland has far more in common with that of the United States than it has with that of Ulster. As well as explaining the decline of sectarianism, we will try to clarify some of the stranger claims that are made about Scotland's supposedly endemic anti-Catholicism. We consider to what extent Scots Catholics now form a distinct homogenous cultural subculture. Finally, we return to the significance of sectarian violence.

Disadvantage and Discrimination

One of our main aims in writing this book is to present contemporary social-scientific evidence about various indices of social disadvantage. It is surely no accident that the lists of those who think Scotland is still an endemically sectarian society are led by a musician, a novelist and a professor of literature – all untouched by evidence beyond their personal experience. It is also significant that the few social scientists who insist that Catholics are still the victims of considerable discrimination support their argument with anecdotes drawn heavily from Scottish football. Claims about supposedly widespread social processes must be supported with society-wide statistical data. Those cross tabulations, charts and tests of significance may be hard to enjoy but they are unavoidable if this subject is to be treated seriously.

But equally important is clarity of analytical thought. Throughout this book we have tried to treat carefully each aspect of the assertions that are made. It is particularly important to separate disadvantage, effective discrimination and bigotry. If we wish to show that the first was caused by the second, which was a result of the third, we have to be able to identify and evaluate each on its own.

Some disadvantage is not doubted. The Catholic Irish entered the Scottish labour market at the bottom. The first wave of migrants left Ireland because their conditions were dire. They arrived with no capital and with none of the skills required for the better-paid industrial jobs. The lack of financial resources meant that it was difficult for them to fund the education that would have allowed their children improved access to the labour market. This was to some extent offset by financial help from native Scottish and English Catholics; as Aspinwall points out, not all Catholics in Scotland were poor. At the same time there was considerable hostility to Irish Catholics, especially from those members of the Scottish working class most in competition with the migrants, from parts of the evangelical churches and from native Scots Catholics. There was certainly lots of bigotry.

The mistake that is often made is to assume, without further evidence to the point, that bigotry created effective discrimination, which in turn was the main cause of Irish disadvantage. Malevolence may have had relatively little effect on the economic position of the immigrants. Bigotry may testify to the ill nature of some Scots; we would have to be precise about just what proportion of Scots were bigots. It may also partly explain the social distance between native and immigrant populations, but we have to recall that, in an age when people took religious differences seriously, a degree of separation would have resulted even if the native Scots Protestants had been uniformly pleasant. But such ill feeling as there was may have made little difference to the economic fate of the immigrants, because the bigots were generally impotent. Such influence as they had was routinely trumped by members of the ruling elite who either did not share the bigotry or, if they shared it, gave greater weight to social harmony. The behaviour of Sir John Gilmour (see page 43) is a good example.

Comparison with Northern Ireland is instructive here. In Northern Ireland bigotry was more effective in ensuring social closure because there were fewer but larger employers with no shortage of labour. Hence they could afford to indulge the preferences of their workers and, once they had been indulged, the resulting preferential employment policies had a great effect. There were also, of course, much bigger political issues that divided Protestants and Catholics. Unionist politicians either deliberately or by inaction allowed the state to become ethnically defined. Their reasoning was that Irish nationalists had been given three-quarters of the island: the Protestants were entitled to their bit. Catholics were denied access to certain sorts of public resources and deliberately opted out of the competition for others. In Northern Ireland, cultural differences, social distance, labour-market access, political preferences, access to public goods and support for the state all reinforced each other in a vicious cycle that deepened the divisions. In contrast, anti-Catholic Scots could huff and puff but they lacked the power (or, if they had it, chose not to use it) to make the state a Protestant resource. Hence bigotry as an attitude did not become enshrined in a social structure.

The first few generations of Irish Catholics laboured under disadvantages (in particular lack of capital and industrial skills) that had nothing to do with sectarianism. The state put few (and arguably no) obstacles in the way of them gradually overcoming those disadvantages. Their fate was not a distinct one that they acquired and kept by virtue of being Catholics; it was one they held in common with non-Catholic poor people. The question then is whether they were handicapped in the race for upward social mobility, either by their own characteristics or by obstacles being put in their way. If we are right in our reading of the evidence presented in Chapter 3, something close to parity has now been achieved. If that is so, it is likely that Catholics worked their way out of poverty at a rate not much slower than that for poor non-Catholics.

The explanation for any lag may well lie with the Catholic Church. Naturally the Church was interested in ensuring that its children remained in the faith and it saw schooling as essential to indoctrination: if we cannot teach our children correct doctrine, Protestants will teach them heresy. The Church's preference for its own system of schooling might be seen as a defensive response to the missionary intentions of the majority, but the Church's theory of education is clear enough, as its history of institution building in places where Catholics are not a precarious minority. Its preference for maintaining effective ways of socialising its children exists quite independently of the hostility of others. It was the Church's decision not to follow the three Presbyterian churches into the embrace of the state education system created by the 1872 Act. The subsequent response of the state is important. It did not declare that the Church had made its own bed and could lie on it. Instead it continued to support Catholic schools and to seek an acceptable way of incorporating them in the state system. That the 1918 Education Act was described as 'Rome on the Rates' by bigots such as Alexander Ratcliffe does not change the fact that the Act gave the Church a settlement more favourable than it had achieved in any other polity and more favourable than that offered to the Presbyterian churches. It was funded on a par with state schools but retained control over staff hiring and curriculum. That Catholic schools continued to perform less well than state schools until comprehensive reform in the 1960s was a reflection, not of anything the state did, but of the greater poverty of its pupils.

We are not asserting that Catholics never suffered discrimination. There is no doubt that some factories in some places practised a preferential hiring policy that gave advantages to non-Catholics. Informal recruitment in small units will always permit nepotism. However, the historical record contains little good evidence of large-scale exclusion.[2] There is certainly little evidence of Catholics being excluded from entire sectors of employment. At the risk of stating the obvious, we should add that easy access to the higher reaches of many professions has often been allowed only to the sons and (much later) the daughters of people who already occupy those positions. We live in a class society and the upper classes use their inherited wealth and social networks (such as those provided by private schooling) to pass their advantages to their children. That excludes the majority of non-Catholics as much as it excludes Catholics. It may be unpleasant but it is not especially sectarian, though it explains why Catholic advance in some small fields is slow. For most routes to upward mobility, whatever the extent and effect of nepotism (and it would not have been great where there were sufficient alternative sources of employment), it was eroded by two things: the decline of the local family firm and the growth of state employment. Both had the effect of increasing the importance of universal criteria such as educational credentials. The local Orange Lodge had some influence over hiring in the dye works of the Vale of Leven in the 1880s. It had little influence over the recruitment policies of the US-owned Timex factory that replaced them in the 1950s and no influence at all over the hiring at the 'silicon-glen' plants of the 1980s.

The Decline of Bigotry

It is incontestable that anti-Catholic bigotry has declined: people who voice what were commonly expressed hostile attitudes in the 1850s now find themselves punished. The extent of intermarriage is a clear indicator of rapprochement. Our explanation of increased civility rests on two separable things: the *decline of religion* and the *loss of power*.

For reasons we would not try to explain here, Britain (like most of the Western world) has become thoroughly secular.[3] Very few people are committed Christians and most of those would share the now-widespread view that religion should not be taken too seriously and should not be allowed to dominate the public world. This cuts the legs out from under anti-Catholicism in three ways. First, there is a general lack of interest in religious identities: quarrels about the best way to attain salvation are irrelevant to most Scots. Second, as the committed Protestant population has shrunk, so the chances of the average Orangeman or Ulster Unionism-sympathising working-class Glaswegian being religious also decrease. Hence that part of the population most likely to behave badly no longer gets the religious legitimation to encourage it in its actions. Witness the lack of clergy support for the anti-Catholic parties of the 1930s or the post-Second World War Orange Order. Third, the contraction of the faithful raises the stakes for theological anti-Catholics such as Pastor Jack Glass. They find that their evangelical witness is compromised by being associated in the public mind with drunken hooligans. So they give up. Although the core of Free Church people presumably have not changed their theological view that the Pope is the anti-Christ, they no longer express bigoted views or act on them. Furthermore, they come to find that they have more in common with conservative Catholics (who at least believe some of what they believe) than they have with 'secular' militant Protestants. We cannot imagine ten, let alone fifty, Free Church ministers now following the example of their great-grandfathers and petitioning to deny a Catholic a senior post in the NHS. And we come back to intermarriage: in a secular society religious upbringing has little impact on social networks.

Then there is the loss of power. We assume some regular connection between how people view the world and their practical experience of it. The two do not always go together; social myths can be powerful (as we saw in the discrepancy between the experience of discrimination and the belief in its existence). But, if a group of people are enduringly unable to put their beliefs into practice, they are unlikely to be able to interest their children in them. The point is perhaps clearer the other way round. Ideas are more plausible when they work than when they do not. White supremacist ideas were more popular and more easily passed on to children in a setting such as Virginia in 1920, where there were real material benefits to be defended and where the obviously inequitable social structure demanded justification, than they were in Virginia in 1990. We can see this very clearly in those settings where ideas have to be formulated and analysed and are then faced with a severe test: constructing party political programmes, for example. In Northern Ireland Ian Paisley's Democratic Unionist Party has succeeded electorally by presenting itself as a Protestant party for a Protestant people. In Scotland Ratcliffe and Cormack failed to make the breakthrough to national politics because the electorate knew they would fail the electoral test. A militant Protestant was always going to be politically impotent. Anti-Catholicism was a losing hand. Even when the sentiment appealed (as witnessed by Cormack's local election victories), the opportunity structure rendered the preference pointless (as the voters recognised when they did not vote for him for a Westminster seat). In a more general way, attitudes changed because the social realities proved unconducive. In Northern Ireland, anti-Catholicism was effective; hence it remained popular. In Scotland it was impotent; hence it declined.

There are a number of causes of Protestant impotence. The most obvious one is that Scotland was not a nation state. It was a small part of the British state and had little autonomous political power. Or, to be more precise, though it enjoyed considerable administrative autonomy, it did not allow much direct democratic influence. As we noted with the example of Scottish Unionist inability to campaign against denominational schools because the English Tories were in favour of them, even if all Scottish Unionists had been avowedly anti-Catholic (and most were not), they would have regularly been trumped by English interests.

A further impediment to effective anti-Catholicism was the fact that Scotland was itself culturally fragmented. By the end of the nineteenth century, when the Irish Catholics presented the biggest challenge to a hitherto largely Presbyterian Scots culture, the Scots were themselves divided and the divisions fell conveniently for peace. Those parts of Scotland in which the religious culture was most conservatively Protestant (and hence that could offer the strongest theological justification for wishing to maintain a Protestant public culture) were the parts with the fewest Catholics. The only Education Authority that petitioned against the terms of the 1918 Education Act was that of Caithness, where there were no Catholic schools to be transferred under the terms of the Act! Anti-Catholicism in Caithness was entirely abstract. Those parts of Scotland that had the greatest presence of Irish Catholics (and Ulster Protestants) had a large number of people who were thoroughly secular or liberal in their Protestantism and the conservative Protestants were divided between a number of competing sects.

Social identity is never fixed; it constantly adapts to circumstance. It was always possible that non-Catholic Scots could have pulled together. They could have decided that the external threat was too great to allow their internal differences to prevent the formation of a united front. This is indeed what happened in Ulster, where Church of Ireland and Presbyterian Church Protestants set aside their religious differences to form a common political front against the greater threat of Irish nationalism. But the Irish in Scotland were never numerous enough or sufficiently united behind any political agenda that could scare non-Catholic Scots into a single camp. There never was a powerful Orange vote.[4] This is quite different from the position in Ireland. There the political ambitions of Catholics (one-third of the population in the North and a vast majority in the island as a whole) posed a serious challenge to the political settlement desired by Ulster Protestants. Even had Scots Catholics possessed a distinctive agenda (Reverse the Reformation? Shift Scotland into another state?), few people would have thought they had the power to do it. Hence the failure of anti-Catholics such as White and Cameron to persuade most Scots to support them.

Next we should put into the equation the behaviour of Scottish elites.[5] Crucial opinion leaders in Scotland declined to support anti-Catholic and anti-Irish campaigns. The *Scotsman* and the *Glasgow Herald* did not campaign against Catholicism and often editorialised against those who did. The aristocracy did not support the Orange Order.[6] Nor did the clergy of the major Protestant churches. During the period of White's domination, the General Assembly of the Church of Scotland approved an anti-Irish agenda but, unlike in Northern Ireland, almost no clergymen associated themselves with popular anti-Catholicism. The civil service, the Unionist Party and the trade-union leadership behaved in an even-handed manner. The professional educators of the Scottish Education Department gave a great deal of support to Catholic school managers even during the period when the Church refused to join what they hoped would be a uniform national school system. Even though they had as elected members Church of Scotland clergy and independent militant Protestants, education authorities generally behaved well. To cite just one small example, when in 1919 a Moderate resigned, the Glasgow Education Authority replaced him with the most successful of the unelected candidates: a Catholic Labour representative.[7] Another example of even-handedness is worth mentioning for its timing and its location. In the early 1920s there was still much ill feeling in Scotland towards the southern Irish because of the 1916 Easter Rising: easily read as taking advantage of Britain's involvement in a world war that all democrats should have supported. The location point is that the Vale of Leven had a large Orange and Unionist population. The aim to improve Catholic schools was hindered by a shortage of qualified teachers. Those trained in Ireland were not recognised because the training course was shorter than that in England and Scotland. Yet in 1920 the Dumbarton Education Authority successfully petitioned the Scottish Education Department to allow it to make up the shortfall in Catholic teachers by recruiting those trained in Ireland.[8]

Where others have concentrated on the florid eruptions of street bigotry, we have noted that such outbursts were usually a response to accommodating and inclusive actions by the ruling class. We find very little evidence that the majority of the native gentry and bourgeoisie shared anti-Catholic sentiments and the historical sources offer very little. But, even if we impute to the silent majority the worst possible sentiments, it is important that they did not act on them. Unlike their counterparts in Ulster, the Scottish ruling class did not deepen the divide. Anti-Catholic action remained of low status throughout the nineteenth century and became more so over the twentieth century. Few things more symbolise the difference between Scotland and Northern Ireland than elite support for the Orange Order. Every Ulster prime minister was an Orangeman. Brookeborough and Craigavon were so by conviction. The Eton-educated Terence O'Neill did not have his heart in it, but even he was obliged to join the Order and to flatter its members. Hundreds of clergymen were members of the Order. Very few Scots politicians were ever members of the Order and we can find none after the 1930s. Only four clergymen have been associated with the Order in Scotland since the 1940s; only two of these were Scots Presbyterians and neither was a figure of any standing in the Kirk.

The most important consequence of the absence of deep divisions around religion and ethnicity was the development of a non-confessional Labour movement. In Northern Ireland the constitutional issue was always so pressing that many trade unions formed on confessional lines. The few Labour politicians who did come to the fore, Harry Midgeley, for example, were forced to pick a side. In Scotland Catholics achieved considerable political power through the Labour movement and non-Catholics put Labourist interests before sectarian identities. We can leave a measured judgement to Peter Lynch:

Though much has been written of the development of popular anti-Catholicism in the 1920s and 1930s, with the growth of

Protestant Action, the Scottish Unionist Party's varied attempts to play the Orange card, and the Church of Scotland's declaration to reverse Irish immigration to Scotland, these political activities had little impact on actual public policy in Scotland.[9]

Sex and Sectarianism

All the above suggests that the social forces that underwrote sectarian divisions were always weaker in Scotland than in Northern Ireland and over the twentieth century they became ever more so. The greatest threat to divisive stereotypes is sexual attraction. Serious social conflict prevents people from opposite camps mixing as equals, and, where the occasional strong personal relationship arises fortuitously, the social pressure to conform will force the offending pair to split or to move. Where the social structure cannot exert that degree of pressure, then sexual attraction will corrode the stereotypes. In line with other studies, our Scottish survey shows a clear connection between type of marriage and strength of church commitment. Fifty per cent of those in 'same-religion' couples attend church regularly as compared to just 13 per cent for those in mixed marriages. This could reflect age: both attending church and having a partner of the same religion are more common with the elderly. Or it could be that declining interest in religion is a *cause* of mixed marriage rather than a consequence – people who take their faith seriously being more likely than others to ensure they marry someone like-minded. But there is no doubt about the direction of cause in the effects of mixed marriage on the next generation. One of the best predictors of whether someone in our Scottish survey will be a regular churchgoer is having two parents of the same religion. For example, of those children born to a same-religion couple in the 1940s, 29 per cent still go to church; for mixed marriages in the same cohort the figure is only 14 per cent.

In the decline of sectarianism, the crucial turning point occurs in the dance hall when the Protestant lad asks the Catholic lass 'Are ye dancin?' So how did the Protestants and Catholics end up in the same dance hall?

Scotland was never as religiously segregated as Northern Ireland but a number of changes post-1939 weakened prevailing patterns of association. Wartime evacuation was one such. Almost half the

children of Glasgow were evacuated, most to predominantly Protestant rural areas. And almost half of them were accompanied by
their mothers. Paterson's detailed study of education records show
that, although some difficulty was expected, there was actually very
little sectarian conflict.[10] Catholic children were comfortably slotted
into Protestant families and schools.

By 1944 about one-third of the Scottish population was engaged
in some form of war work. Many thousands of men enlisted in the
services or were conscripted. Although some infantry regiments
initially recruited by area, so few areas were religiously segregated
that service units invariably mixed Catholics and Protestants. Non-
infantry units never had any specific regional identity and even
infantry regiments quickly became mixed as casualties forced reorganisation. For five years many thousands of men were forced to
cooperate in life-threatening circumstances. It may not be true that
'there are no atheists in fox holes', but it is very likely that men under
fire, who rely on their comrades to cover them and to rescue them if
wounded, revise their notions of just which social divisions matter.

Even for those who did not enlist, the war disrupted previous
social patterns. Thousands of women left home to serve in the Land
Army; many thousands who stayed at home took jobs in large
factories with religiously mixed workforces. Some 20,000 women
from the West of Scotland were conscripted and sent to work in
engineering factories in Coventry. Some idea of the scale of the
disruption can be gained from the following data. At the height of
the war, among women aged 18 to 40, 90 per cent of single women
and 80 per cent of married women and widows without dependent
children were in the services or working in industry.[11]

After the war social changes continued the mixing. What the
Luftwaffe started when it bombed Clydebank, the Glasgow City
Council completed when it admitted that it could not rehouse its
people within its boundaries and accepted the need for the new
towns of Irvine, Cumbernauld and East Kilbride. Between 1945 and
1975 some 200,000 people moved out of Glasgow. For many Scots
post-war prosperity brought a radical change of lifestyle that we can
summarise as the decline of the communal. The crowded tenements
gave way to separate private houses. Decline in family size increased
the importance of the married couple and the domestic home. As
homes became more attractive, the public house became less so.

Children have the effect of rooting adults in communal identities. They strengthen family bonds across generations (for example, parents call more on the help of grandparents) and between families (by adding niece/nephew/cousin ties and new interaction opportunities). In a religious community, they also strengthen ties to the church (because of its involvement in family life-cycle rituals and because those minded to be religious need to arrange religious socialisation of children). When the church also maintains a school system, children further tie adults to the church. Adults without children are much freer to experiment with unconventional identities and relationships than are parents. A couple with five children will spend a lot of time in extended family and communal (hence religio-ethnic) activity. A couple with no children are free to socialise with work colleagues (who are more likely than extended family to be of a different religion). Hence for a variety of complicated reasons, the decline in family size, the decline in popularity of marriage and the delay in having children all have the potential to shift interaction from an inherited communal identity to a freely chosen identity.

All the above may seem rather bloodless, so we will try to bring together these themes by describing in some detail the history of a family to whom one of us is related. 'James' was born in 1963 in the Vale of Leven, a strong Orange area. His family were staunch Orangemen and he joined the Lodge as a juvenile. A keen footballer, he became a Rangers fan. Through family contacts he won an apprenticeship as a cooper, a dying trade even then, kept alive only by the Scotch whisky industry. His parents were regular churchgoers but were not strong enough in their faith to pass it on to him and he ceased attending church when he was about 12. He met and married a young Protestant girl who came from a middle-class family. Jane was not religious and had no involvement or interest in Orangeism or football. James gave up the Lodge, not initially because of any great revaluation of his beliefs but because he was too busy socialising with his fiancée and her friends and then, when he thought about it, it just didn't seem that important any more. A crucial juncture: the couple bought a small house in a development peopled by other young upwardly mobile couples working hard to advance the fortunes of their families. He still worked in a skilled trade once-dominated by Orangemen but he now mixed with people from a wide variety of backgrounds, most of whom commuted to work outside the Vale. Thereafter James went to football matches less often. Especially after they had had children, James spent most of his time working to pay the mortgage, improving his house, and playing with his children. Going out with the lads, football training, the ritual of the day up in Glasgow at the match – all were replaced by domesticity. The bond between his job and his Orange background was abruptly fractured when the cooperage he had worked for since leaving school closed. After a variety of other jobs, he eventually found himself repairing barrels again but this time for a small 'heritage' company that combined the real work of making barrels with a sideline in entertaining tourists. While they created some anxiety, his periods of unemployment had a salutary effect on his relations with his wife. As Jane had only two children and her work was a major source of family income, their marriage became much more of an equal partnership than had been the marriages of their parents. Had they lived fifty years earlier, Jane would probably have accommodated to James's values. In a climate of greater gender equality, James became more like Jane. When they could afford it they went abroad on holiday: to France, Spain and Portugal. They preferred the beaches to the churches but their horizons were broadened. James joked about the shrines and the Our Lady of this and that, but any residual suspicion that there was something intrinsically dangerous about Catholicism was gradually eroded.

James's brother began dating a Catholic girl and, when she became pregnant, he married her. For a very short time James, like other members of the family, shunned the couple. But, once the child was born, Jane encouraged contact and James found himself torn between his Orange heritage and his fondness for children. He quickly decided that being a good uncle mattered more to him than historic identities from which he had already become somewhat remote. James's daughter has recently become pregnant to her Catholic boyfriend. A man who once described himself as a true 'Bluenose' now finds himself enjoying the roles of uncle and grandfather to children whose other relatives are Catholics.

Our point is not that mixed marriages make bigotry impossible; it is that they make it more difficult because they raise the price of passing on traditional animosities. In an increasingly secular world, James would have found no support from his wife and her family, their neighbours, or from most of their friends for inflicting on his children, his nephews and nieces, and his grandchildren a divided view of the world in which some of their family were good people and others were bad.

In this brief biography we see many of the elements of the complex changes that have undermined sectarianism in Scotland: the declining influence of organised religion, the decline of the skilled trades that had once supported a tight work-based community, the decline of pub culture, the increasing importance of the private family home, the domestication of men, the role of dormitory housing developments in weakening communal ties, the broadening of cultural horizons and the effect of mixed marriages. Most Scots have benefited from a huge expansion in personal freedom; identities are far less likely to be inherited and to be constraining. Of course, social class remains a powerful influence on our lives. Those of us with secure well-paid jobs have far greater autonomy than those without. But religion and ethnicity are no longer powerful shaping forces; for good or ill, most Scots have been liberated from those.

Personalising the Abstract

It is testimony to the power that the myth of sectarianism exerts on some minds that, even when they essentially agree with the above account, some writers still find something to condemn. Patrick Reilly and James Conroy have held it against non-Catholic Scots that some of the main levers of change have been abstract social forces rather than a Road to Damascus conversion to love of Catholicism. Having conceded that there is 'much in' the view that 'discrimination in housing and employment is of the past', Reilly quite correctly summarises part of our argument as 'social scientists tell us that sectarianism has been undermined, not by changes in mind and heart, but by the unintended, unforeseen consequences of large-scale upheaval'. He then goes on to produce a caricature of the case:

> A man, your sworn enemy from birth, attacks you every time you meet. One day you come across him wearing a straitjacket. 'Look,' he says, 'I'm not attacking you.' It's a relief, of course, but you know that you owe it all to the straitjacket; he hasn't

changed. All the above argument proves is that discrimination has diminished because it can no longer be so extensively practised . . . Catholics will rejoice that the world has changed . . . in their favour, but may remain unconvinced that they are held in greater affection or esteem . . .[12]

Even with allowance for artistic hyperbole, this is improper. First, as Catholics frequently attacked Protestants, the fighting analogy rather muddies the water. The metaphor of one person beating another also exaggerates the disabilities under which Catholics laboured; at worst we are talking about different levels of reward in a single labour market, not masters and slaves. Remove the fancy prose and Reilly is suggesting that most non-Catholic Scots would discriminate against Catholics if they could. His evidence for this, discussed in the rest of the article, is Donald Findlay QC's fondness for sectarian songs. As so often in these arguments, the case is built on the exotic, not the typical.

Reilly is missing the point that even change driven by the purest and most consciously held of motives takes place in a context of social forces. St Paul's dramatic conversion is not typical. Individuals change slowly as they think about what sorts of things they would like to do and what is possible; they accommodate to realities. Some people change faster than others and those who move faster often use external realities as a way of persuading others to follow them. That a moderate Protestant in Leith in the 1930s tries to persuade his Orange pal that there is no point in voting for Cormack in a Westminster election because it would be a wasted vote even if Cormack won does not mean that only the structure of British politics prevented bigotry. It means that the structural constraints provided a resource that encouraged the liberal and constrained the bigot. That decisions were shaped by structural constraints and that some of the major changes in Scottish society were the result of unintended and unanticipated consequences does not mean that non-Catholic Scots were bad people and remain bad people. It just means that this is how social change occurs. There is no other world, outside social structures, in which minds change spontaneously in response only to consciously embraced ideas and sentiments.

But Reilly's point about affection is fascinating because it shows the pickle we get into if we talk about groups and abstractions as if they were our aunt Elsie. We may hold a person in affection but only a racist can have such feelings about an abstraction such as 'Catholics in Scotland'; the same logical error is needed to love an abstraction as is needed to loath it.

What Does the Good Society Require?

'Belonging to the Catholic Irish immigrant community and retaining an Irish identity are largely incompatible with the dominant culture'; in Bradley's approving citing of the work of a colleague, 'the consequences are racism as well as religious and social prejudice'.[13] One of the difficult questions that must be faced in any serious discussion of supposedly awkward or acrimonious relations is the nature of the good society. What is it that we can reasonably expect? We raise this directly to clarify something that has been implicit throughout the text. Our arguments with others have generally taken one of two forms. In places we have argued about evidence and its interpretation. But we have also sometimes challenged the propriety of offering this or that as proof of sectarianism. In those cases what occurred is not at issue; rather we have not been persuaded that what occurred should be regarded as improper.

We need to tread carefully here because we do not want to stray into telling people what the world should be like. Sociologists describe and explain; their views of how the world should run are not necessarily better than anyone else's. We are not moral philosophers and our interest in the implied models of the good society is not that of picking the best. We raise the question because failure to address it at all seems to be behind a lot of the confusion about the extent of sectarianism.

Bradley, Reilly, Finn and others think it is perfectly proper, indeed laudable, for an immigrant minority to maintain and promote its own culture even when, in its religious and political components, that culture is at odds with the views of most natives. We leave aside for a moment the empirical issue of the cohesion of the immigrants and their descendants. They also think that it is racist to be unenthusiastic about autonomous subcultures and to wish for a society that is more, rather than less, homogenous. This is quite in keeping with progressive views on multiculturalism. The 1950s ideal for the immigrant experience was full integration. The modern position is that migrants should be given full access to economic and political resources but be encouraged to maintain cultural distinctiveness.

The difficulty with this version of multiculturalism is that it is often not pursued consistently or to its logical conclusion but is used in a somewhat partisan manner. For example, Bradley criticises Lord Scone for saying 'culturally the Irish population has not been assimilated into the Scottish population . . . there is in the west of Scotland a completely separate race of alien origin practically homogenous'.[14] Scone was factually wrong about homogeneity: intermarriage was never that rare. He was right about 'alien in origin': the vast majority of Catholics in the West of Scotland were of Irish descent. He was wrong about the degree of cultural distinctiveness. Apart from religion (and even in the 1920s many Catholics had only a nominal commitment to the Church) there is little that separated second- or third-generation 'Irish' Catholics from their non-religious neighbours. But, if Scone is racist, how do we separate the cultural distinctiveness that he dislikes from that which Bradley wishes to promote? Or, to put it the other way round, by what sort of logic can we argue that it is quite proper for an immigrant minority to remain culturally distinctive but it is improper for some elements of the host society to hold views that are critical of some elements of that culture? If it is reasonable for the Irish in Scotland to campaign for Irish independence, why is it racist for Unionists in Scotland to campaign against it? Or, in the field of religion, why is it reasonable for the Catholic Church to maintain that Protestants are not fully Christian but unreasonable for conservative Protestants to maintain that Catholicism is a heresy? Bradley campaigns to persuade Scots of Irish descent to describe themselves in the census as 'Irish' but then complains about a few Scots who regarded west-coast Catholics as 'foreign'.

We raise this point, not to judge which of assimilation or multicultural autonomy is preferable, but to clarify slippage in the various uses of the term 'sectarian'. If we are going to make accurate judgements, we need to distinguish just exactly what is being asserted. Those writers such as MacMillan and O'Hagan who wish to depict Scotland as endemically sectarian are often making no claims about forms of behaviour that the term usually denotes: for example, discrimination in politics, the improper allocation of public monies, or prejudice in the labour market. They concede that such discrimination as did exist in the early twentieth century has largely disappeared but they manage to sustain their critical posture by describing both of the following as evidence of sectarianism: opposition to some aspects of a distinctive Catholic culture and opposition to subcultures in general.

We would like to separate out from this tangle a few clear principles. First, it is not sectarian to object on universal grounds to some aspects of a religion's teaching. For example, many people (including many Catholics) have objected to, and campaigned against, the Catholic Church's support for right-wing politics. In Europe in the 1930s the Church supported clerico-fascist movements in Portugal, Spain, Austria, Croatia and Slovakia. In the 1970s many parts of the Church's hierarchy in Latin America sided with military dictatorships. It is presumably not sectarian to dislike the Catholic Church's support for fascism, provided one is equally critical of Protestant churches that did likewise. In brief, we have to allow that there can be non-sectarian grounds for opposing any particular religion. For example, it is only anti-Islamic to object the sexism of much Islamic culture if you tolerate the same sexist behaviour from other religions.

Even more obviously, it is not sectarian to object to all religions alike. For the National Secular Society to argue against state funding of Catholic schools while arguing for separate state-funded Muslim or Protestant schools would be sectarian. But if it objects even-handedly to all state support for religious activity, then it is merely, in the words of the popular advertisement, doing 'what it says on the tin': being secularist. All committed God-believers will dislike secularism but to construe secularism in Scotland as sectarianism is to play silly games with words.

The partisan nature of Bradley, Reilly and Finn's support for a Catholic religious ethos in schools or an 'Irish' dimension to social identity becomes clear if we consider the majority side of cultural distinctiveness. Take the behaviour of the Bairds of Gartsherrie, the family whose mining and iron enterprises are often identified as examples of anti-Irish Catholic hiring policy in the late nineteenth century. A family of committed evangelical Protestants used their personal wealth to promote what they believed to be the true saving faith. They spent considerable sums building churches and employing missionaries. Unless as a matter of principle we are going to say that people should not be able to use their wealth to promote their faith, it is difficult to fault what they did. We can draw a clear line between the public and private. We could say that a councillor who ensured that only his co-religionists were employed by public funds in public service was behaving in a corrupt manner. We could probably readily agree that, after paying whatever taxes the state imposed, the Bairds could give their wealth to whoever they liked. Those two extremes seem clear but the middle ground is less so.

One possible non-partisan explanation for the inconsistency of lauding a Catholic ethos in state-funded Catholic schools but deriding a Protestant ethos in a privately owned factory is to say that size and power distinguish the cases: it is acceptable for a small and weak minority to preserve its culture but improper for a majority to do likewise. If the minority is clearly disadvantaged, we might support a form of affirmative action. If the minority behaves in a discriminatory fashion, we might justify it on the grounds that the impact of such actions on others is far less than if the majority behaved in that way. So allowing Catholic schools to deny senior positions to non-Catholics while denying non-Catholic schools the right to constrain the professional careers of Catholics can be accepted because the first disadvantages few people while the second would disadvantage many. Although the case is rarely put as bluntly as that, this does seem to be the way that most Scots in practice reason about the matter. If a people's preference for their own kind can be seen as defensive (as in the Muslim desire for endogamy or the Catholic Church's preferential teacher hiring policy), it is widely accepted.

Obviously Scotland is not sufficiently wedded to positive multi-culturalism for Reilly, Bradley and Finn, but equally well it has not followed the French tradition of attempting to create an entirely homogenous citizenry. But, wherever one stands on that debate, it is hard to see the current or recent treatment of Catholics in Scotland as displaying any evidence of what ordinary people would regard as intolerance.

That sentence allows us to return to another of the implicit themes of this study. A number of times we have questioned the accuracy of treating Scots Catholics as a block. The above discussion rather takes it for granted that Catholics formed and still form a homogenous group. One possible ground for supposing that is race, but like almost all contemporary social scientists we emphatically disclaim the language of race. There is nothing in the genetic make-up of Catholics descended in some degree from Irish migrants that distinguishes them biologically from Scots. In a blind test of genetic material, no analyst could work out which sample came from Councillor Pat Lally and which from Pastor Jack Glass. The better grounds for treating 'Catholics descended from Irish immigrants' as a separate group are either that they share common cultural features that distinguish them from their neighbours, or that they share the common experience of being treated by others as if they were a distinctive group.

Putting it like that allows us one way of summarising this study. We find little evidence either that Scots Catholics are now objectively distinctive or that many Scots treat them as if they were. There is no major 'descended-from-Irish-Catholics' language, cuisine, dress style, residential preference or leisure activity. Descendants of Irish Catholic migrants are much more likely than other Scots to practise Irish dancing or to belong to the Ancient Order of Hibernians, but very few people do either. Even religion has lost most of its force as a source of difference as the Catholic Church has followed the Protestant churches in rapid decline. There is a separate educational system, but, as the decline in church adherence shows, that is failing to preserve the singular quality that it was created to defend, and Catholic Church officials now frequently defend their schools on the grounds that they teach conservative moral values. We come back again to intermarriage. People show that some quality is vital to them by giving it pride of place in the selection of their marriage partners. That most Scots Catholics are now perfectly happy to consider non-Catholics as suitable spouses tells us that they no longer regard their Catholicism as a paramount part of their social identity. And so to the second point: do non-Catholics treat Catholics as if they were distinctive? Again, the evidence we have presented in previous chapters suggests an answer in the negative.

Conclusion

Scotland was never as sectarian as Northern Ireland and changes in the Scottish economy, polity and society since the late 1930s have reduced the importance of religious and ethnic identity to a point of irrelevance. In 1986 one of us concluded a discussion of sectarianism in Scotland by describing it, in the words of the title of a Peter McDougall play about violence among working-class men in Greenock in the 1960s, as *Just a Boy's Game*. Having examined the same issues with far better social-scientific data than were then available, we see no reason to amend that conclusion.

Urban Scotland has a problem with incivility. Too many men drink too much, take drugs, carry weapons and regard any insult to an easily offended sense of propriety as justification for assault. Some of those thugs sometimes use religion and ethnic origin to divide their impoverished world into them and us. But, as the evidence we presented in Chapter 4 shows, only a tiny fraction of urban Scotland's violence is sectarian. Furthermore, it is very likely that, if sectarian identities were not available, the Jason Campbells of the world would still act out their twisted machismo under some other pretence. The most significant thing about Scotland's very rare sectarian violence (and what distinguishes it from similar behaviour in the US south in the 1950s or Northern Ireland today) is that it is not connected to anything else that matters: it is not one expression of political, economic, social or cultural differences. It is not the visible tip of a huge iceberg of sectarianism, the bulk of which is concealed beneath the water. It is all the iceberg there is.

It takes some time for social realities to undermine social myths. We all have a weakness for stereotypes, for off-the-shelf motifs that we can use to situate ourselves and others and to make sense of our worlds. If nothing else, such myths provide a ready store of anecdotal material from which apposite examples can be drawn. In his contribution to the debate on removing the bar on Catholic clergy sitting in the House of Commons, the Greenock and Inverclyde MP Dr Norman Godman illustrated the discrimination that his wife's Irish Catholic grandparents had suffered as follows: 'In the early 1920s, her grandfather was one of many Catholics in Govan who had to stand watch over the building of a church which, once the contract workers left, was progressively demolished by people deeply hostile to Catholics in that area.'[15] We have tried to find evidence for this story and can find none. It is hard to believe a church could be 'progressively demolished' without the matter becoming notorious and we can find no Catholic church that was built in Govan at that

174 Sectarianism in Scotland

time. We do not doubt Dr Godman's good faith but we suspect that a much less dramatic event has been embellished over the generations with frequent retelling. In Chapter 3 we drew attention to the discrepancy between the expectations of, and the experience of, job discrimination and sectarian violence. Many Scots think these things are commonplace; almost no Scots claim personal experience of them. There are two possible explanations. Either people are forgetting their own experiences of sectarianism or their expectations are shaped much more by social myths than by experience.

We believe it is the latter, but we close this study by repeating the challenge with which we opened it. We are under no illusion that this is the last word on sectarianism but we do believe it the best attempt to date to come to terms with the available social-science evidence. If others wish to maintain that we are wrong, they have to show that we have misinterpreted the evidence or they have to produce some better evidence. If we have achieved nothing else with this study, we will have performed a useful service in clarifying what needs to be done by those who wish to maintain that Scotland is endemically sectarian.

Notes

1. *The Times*, 20 September 1997.
2. We have spent months intensively rereading the research literature that we have studied over two decades and what strikes us now is how often the same source appears. For example, one recent journal article offers as support for its claims of extensive discrimination five citations. Two of them are the original 1943 book by James Handley and his 1964 revision, two are works by sociologist Robert Miles that present no evidence other than that of Handley, and the fifth is Gallagher's excellent Glasgow study, which also relies very heavily on Handley. See P. Walls and R. Williams, 'Sectarianism at work: accounts of employment discrimination against Irish Catholics in Scotland', *Ethnic and Racial Studies*, 26 (2003), p. 635.
3. See S. Bruce, *God is Dead: The Secularization of the West* (Oxford: Basil Blackwell, 2002).
4. With the first-rate data and sophisticated statistical techniques that are sadly lacking from most discussions of Orange influence, Eric Kaufmann has demonstrated that there is no significant correlation between Orange Order density and voting patterns in Scotland, not even in the case of voting for the Scottish Protestant League: E. Kaufmann, 'The dynamics of Orangeism in Scotland: the social sources of political influence in a large fraternal organisation', unpublished paper.

5. Bruce's previous writings on this subject contain an important error of presentation. His desire to demonstrate the value of sociology as a discipline led him to stress the power of unintended consequences of structural features of the Scottish environment and to pass over the relative benevolence of Scottish opinion leaders. His case was not that Scots (most of whom were bigots) were prevented by social structure from being effective bigots; it was that those Scots who were bigots were so constrained. That distinction could have been better made.

6. The insignificant Lord Scone is the only person we can find who associated himself with extreme political anti-Catholicism; the frequency with which he is cited suggests there were few others.

7. *Glasgow Herald*, 24 March 1922.

8. *Glasgow Herald*, 7 February 1920.

9. P. Lynch, 'Catholics, the Catholic Church and political action in Scotland', in R. Boyle and P. Lynch (eds), *Out of the Ghetto? The Catholic Community in Modern Scotland* (Edinburgh: John Donald, 1998), p. 49.

10. L. Patterson, *Scottish Education in the Twentieth Century* (Edinburgh: Edinburgh University Press, 2003), pp. 103–4.

11. *Manpower* (London: HMSO, 1944), p. 32.

12. P. Reilly, 'The Herald Essay', *Herald*, 31 July 1999. Patrick Reilly was a professor of literature at the University of Glasgow and a weekly columnist in the *Herald* during the 1990s.

13. J. Bradley, 'Facets of the Irish Diaspora: "Irishness" in 20th century Scotland', *Irish Journal of Sociology,* 6 (1996), p. 97.

14. Ibid. pp. 85–6.

15. *Hansard*, 1 March 2001, column 1119. We contacted Dr Godman to ask for further details but he did not reply. We also circulated a number of Glasgow Catholic historians to ask if anyone could identify the church. No one could. The closest incident we could find occurred a century earlier: St Andrew's Church was started in 1814 and 'despite damage by hooligans' completed in 1816: A. L. Drummond and J. Bulloch, *The Scottish Church 1688–1843* (Edinburgh: Saint Andrew Press, 1973), p. 141.

Appendix

Table A3.1 Current religion and religion of upbringing, Scotland, 2001 (%)

Current Religion	Religion of upbringing							
	No religion	Christian none	Roman Catholic	Protestant mainstream	Protestant conservative	Christian other	Non-Christian	Total
No religion	89	54	20	32	34	33	7	37
Christian none	4	44	2	3	3	33		5
Roman Catholic	0.5	2	75	1				14
Protestant Mainstream	5		2	63	29			40
Protestant Conservative	1		0.5	1	32			2
Christian other						33		0.5
Non-Christian	0.5		0.5		0.5		93	1
	100	100	100	100	99	99	100	100
	N = 208	N = 63	N = 270	N = 981	N = 54	N = 3	N = 15	N = 1594
Total	13	4	17	62	3	0	1	100

Note: 'Protestant mainstream' is overwhelmingly Church of Scotland with Episcopalians and Methodists; 'Protestant conservative' includes Baptists, Brethren, Christian Fellowships and the various conservative Presbyterian churches; and those who said 'Christian – no denomination', 'Just Christian' and the like are in 'Christian other'.
Source: Scottish Social Attitudes survey

Table A3.2   Catholic Labour councillors, Glasgow, 1909–74

Period	Labour councillor 'events'	Percentage Catholic
1910–14	7	14
1915–19	9	11
1920–24	48	29
1925–29	69	19
1930–34	92	14
1935–39	95	16
1940–44	72	19
1945–49	110	20
1950–54	89	22
1955–59	93	27
1960–64	95	22
1965–69	77	29
1970–74	100	15

Note: An 'event' was defined as when a Labour councillor entered, left or held a seat on the council, perhaps on more than one occasion, within each time period.
Source: The original data were collected by Iain McLean of Nuffield College, Oxford, and supplied by the UK Data Archive, University of Essex.

Table A3.3   Religion of upbringing by age and class, Glasgow, 2002 (%)

Age and class		Roman Catholic	Church of Scotland	No religion	Other religion	All people in household
18–34	Non-manual	41	46	49	56	48
	Manual	59	54	51	44	52
		100	100	100	100	100
	N	*117*	*102*	*47*	*62*	*318*
35–54	Non-manual	31	38	32	50	36
	Manual	69	62	68	50	64
		100	100	100	100	100
	N	*114*	*133*	*25*	*36*	*308*
55+	Non-manual	14	30	25	52	27
	Manual	86	70	75	48	73
		100	100	100	100	100
	N	*108*	*292*	*12*	*27*	*376*

Note: The social grade of the chief income earner in the household was used to infer the social grade of the respondent. The non-manual socio-economic group comprises social grades A, B and C1; the manual group comprises social grades C2, D and E but, in addition, social grade E also includes those on state benefit or unemployed.
Source: NFO Social Research.

Table A3.4   Religion of upbringing by age and class, Scotland and Glasgow City, 2001 (%)

Age and Class		Roman Catholic	Church of Scotland	No religion	Other religion	All People in household
Scotland						
18–34	Non-manual	49	51	44	53	49
	Manual	51	49	56	47	51
		100	100	100	100	100
	N	*203,663*	*423,758*	*295,268*	*187,579*	*1,110,268*
35–54	Non-manual	49	53	45	59	52
	Manual	51	47	55	41	48
		100	100	100	100	100
	N	*278,739*	*762,041*	*180,585*	*239,810*	*1,461,175*
55+	Non-manual	27	34	28	43	35
	Manual	73	66	72	57	65
		100	100	100	100	100
	N	*198,227*	*810,036*	*57,966*	*245,144*	*1,311,373*
Glasgow City						
18–34	Non-manual	43	49	48	49	47
	Manual	57	51	52	51	53
		100	100	100	100	100
	N	*44,312*	*46,048*	*30,390*	*30,586*	*151,336*
35–54	Non-manual	39	42	43	49	43
	Manual	61	58	57	51	57
		100	100	100	100	100
	N	*53,028*	*63,174*	*14,291*	*24,026*	*154,519*
55+	Non-manual	19	26	21	30	24
	Manual	81	74	79	70	76
		100	100	100	100	100
	N	*44,506*	*68,239*	*5,560*	*21,692*	*139,997*

Note: The social grade of the household reference person was used to classify the other adults in the household. The non-manual socio-economic group comprises social grades A, B and C1; the manual social group comprises grades C2, D and E but, in addition, social grade E also includes those on state benefit or unemployed.
Source: GRO Scotland, Census, 2001.

Table A3.5 Experience of crime, Glasgow, 2002

Motive	Physically attacked		Victim of vandalism		Threatened		Victim of other harassment	
		%		%		%		%
Can't say	16	(11)	37	(13)	14	(8)	17	(11)
Area where you live	18	(12)	34	(12)	14	(8)	11	(7)
Football team	14	(10)	3	(1)	5	(3)	3	(2)
Gender	9	(6)	1	(_)	6	(4)	9	(6)
Religion	7	(5)	6	(2)	8	(5)	4	(3)
Sexuality	8	(5)	2	(1)	1	(1)	6	(4)
Country of origin	7	(5)	3	(1)	4	(2)	6	(4)
Age	4	(3)	2	(2)	11	(7)	7	(5)
Race	0	(_)	2	(1)	8	(5)	10	(6)
Skin colour	1	(1)	1	(_)	7	(4)	8	(5)
None of the reasons listed	77	(52)	199	(69)	104	(62)	93	(60)
Total of motives	161	(100)	290	(100)	182	(100)	174	(100)
Total of victims	147		288		168		155	

Source: NFO Social Research.

Table A3.6 National identity and religion, Scotland, 1999 and 2001 (%)

Identity	1999			2001		
	Roman Catholic	Church of Scotland	No Religion	Roman Catholic	Church of Scotland	No Religion
Scottish not British	34	31	37	40	35	38
More Scottish than British	41	40	31	34	31	30
Equally Scottish & British	17	24	19	19	27	20
More British than Scottish	1	2	4	1	3	3
British not Scottish	2	1	5	1	2	4
Other, or none of these	5	1	4	4	1	6
	100	100	100	100	100	100
N	215	514	586	225	598	591

Source: Scottish Social Attitudes survey.

Table A3.7 Religion and political preference, Scotland, 2001 (%)

Political preference	Roman Catholic	Protestant	No religion	Other religion
Did not vote	34	22	41	33
Conservative	0	12	5	5
Labour	51	36	28	29
Liberal Democrat	4	14	9	19
Scottish National Party	5	12	11	7
Other parties	3	1	3	5
	100	100	100	100
N	229	689	592	92

Source: Scottish Social Attitudes survey.

Table A3.8 Labour voting in the 2001 general election by religion and age/class, Scotland, 2001 (%)

Percentage of each group voting Labour	Age group			Social class		
	18–34	35–54	55+	Non-manual	Manual	All
Catholic	29	52	73	50	52	51
N	69	77	79	88	117	225
All others	22	35	36	29	37	32
N	341	495	537	684	554	1,373

Source: Scottish Social Attitudes survey.

Table A3.9 Personal morality, Scotland, 2001 (%)

Do you personally think it is wrong or not wrong for . . .	Always wrong	Almost always wrong	Wrong some-times	Not wrong at all	Can't choose	Total
a man or woman to have sexual relations before marriage	10	5	11	65	7	100
school teachers to explain homosexuality to teenagers	14	8	13	51	13	100
a woman to have an abortion	11	12	37	29	10	100
adults of the same sex to have sexual relations	38	7	10	30	14	100
a married person to have sex with someone other than spouse	59	26	8	2	3	100

Source: Scottish Social Attitudes survey (self-complete supplement *N* = 1,381).

Index

Index 185